Philomena Begley

First published 2017 by The O'Brien Press Ltd,
12 Terenure Road East, Rathgar, Dublin 6, D06 HD27, Ireland.
Tel: +353 1 4923333; Fax: +353 1 4922777
E-mail: books@obrien.ie. Website: www.obrien.ie
The O'Brien Press is a member of Publishing Ireland.

ISBN: 978-1-84717-966-1

8 7 6 5 4 3 2 1
21 20 19 18 17

Printed and bound by ScandBook AB, Sweden.
The paper in this book is produced using pulp from managed forests.

Cover photograph © Getty Images, shows Philomena Begley performing live onstage
at the Country Music Festival, Wembley Empire Pool, 1 April 1976. (Photo by Andrew
Putler/Redferns).

Philomena Begley and the publisher wish to thank the following for permissions to
reproduce song lyrics: John Conway for 'A Village in County Tyrone' and Shunie Crampsey
for 'A Tribute to Billie Jo'; and for permission to reproduce extracts from *Entertainment
News* on pages 120–121 and 135–136, and the photograph of his parents, Tony and Joan
Loughman, on page 69: Anthony Loughman. All other photographs appear courtesy of
Philomena Begley and H&H Music.

Published in

DUBLIN

UNESCO
City of Literature

Philomena Begley

My Life, My Music, My Memories

Philomena Begley
with Emma Heatherington

THE O'BRIEN PRESS
DUBLIN

Dedication

To my mother:
A lady so very rare,
Content in her home and always there.
On earth she toiled, in heaven she rests.
God bless you, Mammy,
You were one of the best.

To my father:
He was a great inspiration to me and always gave me advice.
If ever I had any problems, he told me to handle
them in a diplomatic manner.

Contents

Note from Philomena

Fifty-five years in show business … That's a lot of years to cherish and remember, as well as the twenty years before it as I grew up in Pomeroy in my beloved Tyrone.

I honestly can't tell you how grateful I am for all the years of support, friendship, laughs and adventures you all have experienced with me since I first sang on stage in Ardboe Hall in 1962. It really doesn't feel that long ago, but sure I am still as young at heart as I ever was – still the same Philomena and please God I'll never change.

I thought that now, five years after my jubilee year, it was about time I wrote a few things down before the old memory gets too fuzzy, and I have had such fun recounting and recalling all the faces, places, dates, names, antics and craic along the way! Sometimes it's hard to recall what you did last week, never mind the last millennium, so I hope you'll forgive me if I've left anything or anyone out!

I want to take this opportunity to thank each and every one of you from the bottom of my heart for being such a huge part of my life, and believe me when I say that every single day I cherish this gift I have been given, which stemmed from very humble yet very happy beginnings.

I have had an absolute ball every step of the way, so this book is my gift to you, my loyal fans and friends. This is my story. I hope you enjoy!

Route 65 to Nashville!

17 March 1978, New York City

1978 was a year that I will never forget, for bringing me to the highest of highs in my career, and to the lowest of lows in personal loss, and as I walked this street in New York City on St Patrick's Day, I can honestly say I had never seen anything like it in my whole life.

Everywhere we looked, from the moment we arrived at the airport a few days earlier, we saw green. I have always been very well used to the colour green, having grown up surrounded by the rolling hills and mountains around the Irish village of Pomeroy, but this was a different way of seeing green altogether.

Pints of beer were green, animals were painted green, women wore suits of green, and despite the bitter cold, thousands of green faces lined the streets and cheered us along 5th Avenue where we walked, a long, long way from home, as part of one of the world's biggest celebrations of being Irish.

I was marching behind the bands in the parade as one of the Top Rank Entertainment Stars with Omagh-born singer Brian Coll (of the Buckaroos fame), and we couldn't believe our ears, or our eyes. Top Rank Entertainments were Ireland's biggest country music management team at the time, led by Tony Loughman of Castleblayney, County Monaghan (a town that was known back then as Ireland's own Nashville), and we had been selected to represent them in one of the most famous cities in the world.

Brian and I both wore green blazers and cream trousers to take part in the parade, but I was also decked out in snazzy high heels, not having the brains to know that walking seven miles in them in the freezing cold wasn't going to be the best idea I'd ever had! It didn't take me long into the parade to catch on to my big mistake, for I was in pure agony the whole way, but I smiled and waved the whole way through, never letting on how much pain I was really in.

I have to say it takes a lot to faze me in life. I try not to let things overwhelm me and if they do, I never do let on, but looking back, being part of such a magnificent event in America really was magical and it was such a huge honour to be there. I remember looking over at Brian, who was on the other side of the parade, and we smiled with massive pride at the very idea of being there.

The next day, further south in the USA and in shorts and T-shirts hot weather, we were picked up at the airport in Nashville, Tennessee, by honky-tonk singer-songwriter Hank Locklin, who arrived to get us in a pick-up truck. I was there to record at Fireside Studios with the famous Porter Wagoner, who was known as Mr Grand Ole Opry and for whom Dolly Parton wrote the song 'I Will Always Love You'. Porter was one of Nashville's top record producers. And I had to pinch myself to realise that Hank Locklin of 'Please Help Me, I'm Falling' fame had actually picked us up and that we were on our way to make music history in one of the highlights of my country music career, which I believed had happened by chance. Imagine a wee girl from the hills of Pomeroy in County Tyrone, travelling with a real American country superstar! I still can't believe it till this very day, and I don't know if I ever will.

Enjoying the St Patrick's Day Parade in New York City, 1978.

I sat in the front of the truck with Hank while my husband Tom Quinn, Brian Coll and Kevin Ward, a manager from our record company, climbed onto the back – what a memorable way to drive into Music City! I remember the boys laughing their heads off as we drove through the streets with the three of them clinging to the back of the pick-up as if they were going to fall out if Hank braked too suddenly!

Hank dropped us off at the Hall of Fame Motel, right up on the old Music Row, which was just walking distance from the studio where I was to record for the coming week. It was the first time I had seen a king-sized bed and such fancy décor, and I couldn't believe we were staying next door to the famous Country Music Hall of Fame and Museum. Right in the middle of all the action! As far as places to stay in Nashville came, this was most definitely the 'in place' to be and convenient for everything we needed.

St Patrick's Day in New York City had been out of this world, and it looked like Nashville was going to be too. Music was coming out of all corners: rooftop bars, outdoor bars, street music; you name it, they were playing it. I certainly felt far from the tiny Irish streets of Pomeroy where I had spent all of my life until then. Nashville was by no means as commercial in 1978 as it is now, but it was still awfully impressive, with its bright lights, sights and smells and we were there to do a very important job with some very important people. Big-name session musicians like Bobby Dyson (bass), Hargus 'Pig' Robbins (piano), Fred Newell (electric guitar and banjo), Weldon Myrick and Sonny Garrish (steel guitar), Terry McMillan (strings), Dave Kirby (acoustic and rhythm guitar), Joe Chrisman (drums) and Laverna Moore, Curtis Young and Becki Foster doing backing vocals.

With Porter Wagoner at Fireside Studios, Nashville, 1978.

We settled in to our hotel and it was down to business from the moment we hit Fireside Studios, to record not one, not two, but three studio albums!

One day during recording, Porter Wagoner took me for lunch in a wee shack across from the studio. It was a humble enough wee spot and I didn't expect to see anyone out of the ordinary, so you can imagine how my heart nearly stopped when I saw George Jones, the Texas singer of 'He Stopped Loving Her Today' and often referred to back then as 'the greatest living country singer'. 'The Possum', as he was also known, was and still is my biggest music idol, and there he was in the very same café as me! It was nearly like seeing the man above himself! Porter introduced us and I can't for the life of me remember what I said, but I do recall that the man with George knew who *I* was, much to my surprise.

'You recorded "Blanket on the Ground"?' he said to me.

I'd had a big hit with the song in Ireland not long before, so I nodded and, again, I have no idea what I said in response.

'I wrote that song,' he said.

'You actually wrote it?' I said, eyes wide like a modern-day teenager meeting a boy band.

'I sure did,' he replied, and I couldn't believe it. The man with George Jones was Roger Bowling, who wrote the song that had put me on the music map in the UK and Ireland. Well, you could have knocked me down with a feather. It was 'Blanket on the Ground' that gave me my first really famous hit, so you could say that it was his song that had brought me to this spot, standing in front of its creator.

* * *

Saturday night in Nashville was known as Opry Night then, and there was a radio show that gave visiting artists a chance to perform on the big stage itself. I tried not to think about it too much, but I was just about to be the very first Irish female artist to sing on that stage, and it proved to be the most surreal thing I have ever experienced. I stood there in the wings with Hank Locklin and Skeeter Davis, who reassured me that any nerves I was feeling were a very good sign. Porter Wagoner introduced me on stage as I stood there shaking.

'Ladies and gentlemen,' he said to the audience. 'Please welcome my friend from Ireland, Miss Phil-eena Begley!'

Phil-eena? I had to laugh. I had been called many variations of my name down the years, but Phil-eena was definitely a new one!

The audience were of course none the wiser that he'd pronounced my name incorrectly, because they had no idea who I was anyway. But boy, it was some feeling to walk out onto that stage, nervous or not. I was wearing a white satin dress and I thought I was 'no miss' (where I come from, that means you feel on top of the world), but looking back, I don't think the dress was as nice as I thought it was! I suppose it was fashionable back in the day, even with the home-made belt I'd wrapped around my waist, but to this day it still makes me cringe when I think of it! Everyone else still loves it though, so maybe I'm being too hard on myself and my fashionable creations!

I looked out into the audience as the band struck up the intro to 'Blanket on the Ground', reluctant to say very much to the crowd because I was afraid they wouldn't understand me.

'I can't understand one word you are saying when you talk, Philomena,' Porter Wagoner used to joke with me when we were recording. 'Yet when you sing, I can pick up on every word.' This seemed to be a solution for us both, so during our conversations from then on, he'd ask me to sing what I was trying to say to make things easier for him, and it worked!

I finished the song, and took my bow and left the stage to meet Porter in the wings. He was urging me to go back on. I was on such a high from the loud applause of the audience that now *I* didn't have a clue what *he* was saying.

'They want more,' he said to me.

'More?' I asked.

'Yes, Phil-eena, they're giving you an encore. You're getting an encore in the Grand Ole Opry. Now, go give them some more!'

I peeped out from the wings to where the audience was on its feet. Porter was right. To my total surprise, they were cheering and clapping and chant-ing for an encore. They really did want more! By this stage in my career, I'd played many big venues closer to home – places like Wembley with Ray Lynam, where we'd received many encores – but we were never allowed to go out and give a crowd more, no matter how much they asked for it. Maybe there was never time for it, or maybe in England we were consid-ered a small-time act compared to the big American acts. Yet right here in Nashville, right in the heart of Music City, I was being told to go back out and give them some more. An extremely rare thing for an unknown artist like me.

My heart pounded with disbelief and my hands were shaking as I took to the stage one more time, and I gave the rapturous crowd another shorter rendition of 'Blanket on the Ground'. Hank and Skeeter smiled from the side of the stage. Porter seemed to understand me very well when I sang that song, so he smiled too, and he and Hank smiled at each other in approval.

I had just been given an encore in Nashville, and it was going to take a long time to sink in, but I knew there was no way I was going to tell that story when I got back home to Tyrone. It wasn't that they wouldn't have believed me – I just didn't want anyone to think I was blowing my own trumpet, or 'bumming and blowing' as they say around home. At home I was just Philomena Begley, the bread-man's daughter who happened to do something a wee bit different for a living.

Home to me was in Pomeroy, a little village in County Tyrone, a place where my own people would always keep my feet firmly on the ground. There was no way I would ever have notions of myself, as they say where I come from, and that's just how I've always liked it.

Chapter One

A Village in County Tyrone

I was dreaming last night of old Ireland,

A place where I once had a home.

Not in Dublin, Killarney or Derry,

But a village in County Tyrone.

'A Village in County Tyrone', Jack Conway

I was christened Kathleen Philomena Begley, and I came into the world on Tuesday, 20 October 1942, delivered at home in the hilltop rural village of Pomeroy, County Tyrone, by a lady known as Nurse Loy.

Elsewhere in the world, Bing Crosby was topping the charts with 'White Christmas', Churchill was in power in Britain, Ireland was in the midst of the Emergency and Eamon de Valera was the Taoiseach. Life in rural Ireland was simple and honest, and the Begley family lived at the 'top o' the town', where Gaelic football and céilí music were at the heart of the community.

I was the fourth of the Begley clan to arrive, born after my brother Patsy and my older sisters Annette and Mary. Angela came soon after me, then Plunkett, then Margaret, and six years after Margaret came 'the wee late one', Kieran, making eight of us in total. My father, Joe Begley, was a bread-man from the Main Street in Pomeroy. He hadn't had to travel far to find himself a bride, as my mother Josie (née Rafferty) was from just around the road in the townland of Gortnagarn, where I spent many childhood summers on my 'holidays'. My father played accordion so ours was a home full of music for as far back as I can remember.

My grandfather, Patrick Bigley, owned a grocery shop where customers bought their tea, meal, oil and sugar by the weight. I never did find out why my grandfather spelled his surname differently to how we did, and it's something I often wonder about. A lot of people thought I had made a change when I became a singer, but I can assure everyone that it was not my idea at all. Though at one point I was asked to change my name to my christening name, Kathleen, as it was thought to be easier to remember. I refused to do so. I wanted to stay Philomena Begley. Maybe someone somewhere thought 'Bigley' wasn't swanky enough, but they can't pin that one on me!

My maternal grandparents, Edward and Sarah Ann Rafferty, both passed away very young, before my mother was fifteen years old, so I didn't know them at all, and I suppose this made me appreciate my Granny and Grandad Bigley all the more.

My father owned a small farm in the nearby townland of Limehill, known as The Curragh, and things were good despite the difficulties of the outside world, which we were mostly oblivious to. I can happily say that not one of us ever went without. Pomeroy is a rural little village in the middle of County Tyrone, in the townland of Cavanakeeran, where everyone knows your name and who you belong to. It was a lot like most small Irish villages of the time really, and I have many fond memories of a totally blissful childhood there.

Neither of my parents drank alcohol; there was no such thing as drugs, of course, unless you counted a bit of tobacco; and our house was always filled with laughter, song and a clatter of noise – I suppose what else would you expect with eight of a family all squeezed into a three-bedroom terraced house?

My mother, Josie, was always a very hard worker. She would milk 'the Molly Cow' twice a day, as well as looking after everything else that went on around her. I was never sure if Molly was the cow's name or if 'the Molly Cow' was the breed of the animal, but that's what we called her anyhow, and she always gave us plenty of milk, no matter how many of us were there to drink it!

We had a scullery, a sitting room and three small bedrooms in our house on the Main Street, in a part of the village known as 'the top o' the town'. All five of us girls shared a good big bedroom with two double beds. When our cousins, Mary, Celine and Pat Quinn, came to stay, we'd 'top and tail', as we called it, with heads and toes peeping out at each end of the bed.

When I was very young, I loved to help out at my Granda Bigley's shop across the road, and I often went out on the delivery run with my uncle Eugene. I filled oil for customers, lifted eggs, came home and cleaned them for the shop, weighed the meal, tea and sugar, cut the bacon and measured out what customers wanted, which was nearly always the same thing every time for every customer. There were no fancy ways of feeding back then, and in their weekly shop most people ordered a quarter of butter or margarine, a half a pound of bacon, a quarter of tea and a pound of sugar.

Granny Bigley was a fine woman, and lived until she was 100 years old. She liked us all to help out on the weekends. I'd try to convince my sister Angela to do my shift on a weekend, so I could have a lie-in after singing the night before, but it was always the same ritual.

'Angela, will you do my turn at Granny's tomorrow so I can have a lie-in?' I'd ask her.

'Not a chance,' she'd say.

I'd keep begging and begging, but she'd always give the same response until money was mentioned.

'I'll give you ten shillings if you do,' I'd say to her, knowing that would work a treat.

'Give me it now then,' she'd tell me, with her hand out. She always made sure she got the money up front, in case her end of the bargain didn't come through as promised!

Granny would have weighed everything in the shop, from peas to raisins, tobacco and sugar. You could buy War Horse tobacco or a ten pack of Woodbines, and she even sold cigarettes by the singles. In our early teens, we used to go down to the forest, which was known as 'the planting', to have a sneaky smoke. I'd borrow some money from the till and put it in my shoe. Then we'd go to Bannon's shop, where we thought we wouldn't be recognised, to get our supplies. The lady behind the counter was a bit short-sighted, but she knew fine well who we were!

At home, Mammy would make us porridge for breakfast, and the hard bread left over from my father's van was used for 'bread boily', a kind of bread and butter pudding with raisins, milk and sugar. When there was no sugar, we'd use syrup in our tea, and I remember how it used to turn the tea black.

I remember one day when one of the hens had taken my bread off me. My neighbour, Marita Devlin, told the story many years later of how I said, 'The hens ate my sodie sarl,' meaning a soda farl, but it was more likely the other way around – I probably took it from the hens!

Like most families of the 1940s and 1950s, when it came to food we'd waste nothing, and Mammy always made sure we never went short. There'd be a bit of beef on a Sunday, with spuds and a few basic vegetables that we grew ourselves, and I remember one time a neighbour of ours, Tommy Devlin, killed a hare by accident and Mammy cooked it. None of us knew what it was we were eating. My brother Plunkett was clearly enjoying it, because he asked for more 'rat' mid-chew, thinking it was some sort of rodent we were feasting on! We really hadn't a clue what it was, but it tasted all right and it was a good sign when Plunkett was asking for more. We definitely weren't fussy eaters and I don't remember anything too extravagant coming our way for dinner, but I don't remember ever going hungry, so it must have been all right.

My parents, like many Irish couples with big families back then, both had to work very hard to keep us all happy and to keep everyone fed and clothed. Mammy worked in the home, and had plenty to do to look after us all. She had a washboard and a mangle for our clothes, and we helped her by wringing out the blankets and hanging them up wherever was clean and dry, which could be on the grass or over a hedge outside. There were no fancy washing lines back then, and the work was heavy and not always practical with so many children, but Mammy was a real lady and she never raised her voice or said 'boo' to anyone. Nothing seemed to bother her, despite having so much to do. She just seemed to get on with it.

My father, Joe, was a very well-respected man in the wider Pomeroy community. He started the Pomeroy Accordion Band, so music always filled our home, and I can still hear him singing around the house. He also brought the credit union to Pomeroy and, with Ernie Stewart and the local farmers, he set up the local sales yard. He was a passionate GAA man, and he was heavily involved in both the club and county teams. My uncle Packie, or 'The Poke' as he was known on the field, played football for Tyrone. I remember one day there was a fire in Margaret Trainor's ice cream shop, and the team, who had been training in the local hall, came

With my mammy and daddy in Bundoran in the late 1970s.

to help put it out. Our life was simple and lovely, and I remember always thinking that as long as Daddy was around, nothing or no-one would ever hurt us. He was the boss, although very placid and hard-working, and he always made our home feel very, very safe.

We'd all play our part around the house, gathering spuds and turf or watching the wee ones. There were no playpens to keep children in the one place, so we had a big tea chest from Grandad Bigley's shop, which had the nails hammered well down, and it kept the wee ones out of trouble. I remember Margaret and Plunkett in it, and there was a good chance I was in it before they came along too.

Bath night was once a week, in a tin bath in front of the fire. We were all washed in the same water, and had our hair rinsed with an old tin can of freezing cold water, which they said put a shine to your hair, but I think it was to kill the bugs!

We'd say the rosary every night. We'd all have to take our turn in saying a decade each. I used to try and dodge saying mine all the time, and Patsy would have us all in stitches – even Daddy would end up laughing his head off by the time we were finished.

All of us brothers and sisters had our own personalities, and we each liked to be heard when we got the chance. Patsy, the eldest, was the life and soul of the house, a real comedian, who could make a bit of fun out of nothing. He was a very premature baby, weighing only about 2 lb when he was born, and rumour has it that our aunt, when she came to visit, used to warm him by the oven, thinking he needed a bit of incubation at home. I'm not sure how that worked, if at all! It didn't take much to annoy our neighbour, Mrs McElhone, who had a wee pond near her home. There was a wall beside her house and we used to scrape along it with a stone, which drove the poor woman mental. One day, Patsy was accused of throwing stones at the ducks in her pond, and he got a smack for it and was put to bed.

Annette was very quiet and modest. She liked to keep a good eye on all her things, which was never easy with so many brothers and sisters. She was a home bird and she was Daddy's right-hand woman. She even drove the bread van when she was old enough – the only female bread delivery person around. Mary was a bit of a tomboy, and very outgoing. She loved to run the roads, and never missed the swingboats when they came to town.

Meanwhile, Angela and Plunkett would be up to no good, just for the laugh too. I remember Angela, who was fond of her grub, being caught drinking baby Plunkett's bottle around the side of the house when Angela was about five or six years of age. Plunkett could have turned his hand to anything. He was such a hard worker, and apart from the odd wee harmless bit of devilment, you wouldn't have heard his word.

Like most siblings, it didn't take much for us to start a row between us. One day Angela and I tugged on a blouse until it tore, so neither of us got the wear out of it in the end. Margaret was pleasant, modest and caring, while Kieran was spoilt rotten, being the baby and the youngest. He got a lot of attention from his older siblings, especially me!

Saturday was clean-up day. We'd all muck in, cleaning out the presses and washing down the sofas or cleaning out the back. There was always something to do and, thankfully, there were plenty of us to do it.

* * *

We loved visiting Minnie Nugent's for sweets or Conway's Shop, where we'd go with our coupons in exchange for our bits and pieces.

One of my earliest memories of growing up in Pomeroy was hearing and seeing aeroplanes going overhead and not knowing where they were going, or what they even were for that matter. Looking back, I now know they were war planes, of course, and would probably have been coming and going from the aerodrome at the village of Ardboe near Lough Neagh, about eighteen miles away from us. The airbase was the home of 3,500 American troops, a rest stop for bombing crews during the Second World War, and it was a big deal for a rural area such as Cookstown to host so many new people back then. By 1946 they had all left, so I could only have been three or four when I saw those planes flying above our tiny village.

Another early memory for me is the big snow of 1947, when I was just five years old. I remember coming out of the house and watching my father leave to deliver the bread on a sleigh, helped by Uncle Peter and some of the neighbours. The snow was so high that I thought it went on for miles and miles above my head.

Locals would gather in Pomeroy on fair day, normally on a Tuesday, and they would sell cattle and horses on the street. Strangers would come in to buy and sell too, and the fair always attracted plenty of characters. There used to be a man who would go around the fair singing at the top of his voice and our Mary would follow him doing the same. Sally the Bottle was another local character. Sally wore a brown outfit, and always had boxes and bottles under her coat, for reasons that I do not know. Her real name was Sarah McElhatton and I have no idea what she did with all her belongings, but 'Sally the Bottle' was a name that stuck, and everyone in the village knew her! The locals liked to wind her up. I remember Tommy

Devlin popping his head around our kitchen door one day saying:

'Would you sell your donkey for tuppence, Sarah?'

Sally the Bottle didn't take his words too kindly. She lifted her stick and hit the light switch in our kitchen, breaking it instantly. It was the only room we had electricity in, and it was a big deal to get it fixed, but Sarah didn't seem to care. When Mammy would feed her, Sarah would lick the plate. She always had ginger biscuits with her and she'd give us some if we were good. Her hands were always almost black with dirt, but we'd eat from them anyway. Patsy shot a pellet gun from the bedroom window one night, and it caught Sarah on the backside. She went straight up after him and he climbed out the window and away down the garden, laughing his head off, knowing if she caught him, he'd be in big trouble.

Every fair day, we washed the dishes in Granny's café, and helped get everything ready for the farmers who would stop in the café for their tea. The fair was a big occasion in the village. There would be stalls selling everything from clothes to food to bits and bobs for the house. I loved watching all the comings and goings and the characters that the fair brought to Pomeroy.

We passed many of our childhood days in Pomeroy on the railway tracks, jumping along the rails until the trains got close. We also played old games like skipping and hopscotch. Sunny days were spent sliding down McGahan's garden on a sheet of cardboard, and I remember Rosaleen Casey tore her dress and Mammy had to sew it.

Mammy was brilliant on the sewing machine, an old black Singer with pedals on it. She used to steep old Early Riser flour bags until the black-bird logo on them would fade off, and then she would sew them together to make sheets. We'd make tents from sheets on the bed – we had a very old-fashioned four-poster bed, and we'd tie the sheets up and play there for hours.

One of our favourite pastimes was to hold concerts in Harte's Yard. We would charge a penny in, and we'd even have special guests, such as local woman Annie Tally. Mind you, most of the time Annie was the only audience we had, so we didn't make a lot of money from our talents!

Another of our regular games was to tie a piece of thread to the door knocker of Maggie Ford's house across the road, and hide as we pulled the thread. One time, though, when I tied the thread from one door knocker to the other, the local constable came along on his bike and it took his hat off when he rode into it! The road we lived on at the 'top o' the town', was very busy, and sometimes dangerous. Margaret was once knocked down by a car, and another day Angela was saved by a man sweeping the streets when a bus almost ran her over. So tying thread across such an unsafe road wasn't really a very wise idea!

I liked to mop the floors, and sometimes I was a bit generous with the water I'd use. Margaret McConnell, a family friend, said to me one day:

'That floor will never dry, Philomena.'

My response, which my family often quote back to me now, was:

'Margaret, "never" is a very, very long time.'

I've believed in and lived by that motto ever since, as much as I can considering things possible and achievable.

* * *

My springtimes and summers were spent in one of my favourite places in the world, which was just a few miles from home but it sometimes felt like a different world to me. It was the house of my aunt Annie Quinn and her family, in the townland of Gortnagarn. I'd stay there for weeks at a time. Annie had three daughters, Mary, Celine and Pat, and we were all best buddies. There was a barn at their house, and a lovely garden with a pump for water outside the door. In spring, we would build what we called 'Easter huts'. We'd carry water from the well and roll eggs down the hill, while Aunt Annie made soda bread and fried eggs on the pan. The pan was set on top of an old coal bucket, and you'd have to pick your corner to get fed! She had a big pot in which she boiled spuds for her hens, but sometimes the poor hens didn't get them if we got to them first!

On a late August evening in 1954, in the village of Ardboe, a lady called Teresa Grimes was standing in her home when she experienced a vision of the Mother of God standing in a bush at the bottom of her garden. More visions followed in other parts of the country, and people were keen to see one for themselves. We were no different, even though I was only twelve years of age. So my cousins and I would spend days and days in a field in Gortnagarn, praying at a lovely bush in the front garden, hoping that the Blessed Virgin Mary would appear to us! We were totally convinced that we would witness an apparition if we sat there long enough, but needless to say it didn't happen. I still wonder if we weren't praying hard enough!

One of our favourite games was Doctors and Nurses. We would come up with all sorts of illnesses to report, not even knowing what half of them meant. For some reason, I always seemed to be the patient – my sisters and cousins reckon it's because I always loved being cared for.

We used to sing 'Good Companion' together for fun. One night in the bathroom, the leg fell off the bath while we were singing and acting the eejits, and it nearly came through the bathroom floor. We'd also make a dam in the river at Gortnagarn to make our own swimming pool.

We had to make our way across stepping stones in the river, over the gate at the railway, and up the steep hill at Ramsay's Field to get to mass in the mornings. We'd follow Aunt Annie, as she walked with her hands behind her back, all the way to the chapel. She used to tell us if we walked the same as her, with our hands like that, it would give us brains! And we would walk for miles and miles all around the outskirts of the village, with no concern for safety whatsoever.

In winter, there'd be snow and frost and we'd throw a bucket of water out on the street so that it would freeze up and form the perfect slide. My sister Mary lost a tooth one day when she fell on that ice. But I'm surprised there weren't more accidents, as there were no gritters on the road and our buckets-of-water slides made it very, very slippery!

They were gentle, happy times in a quite simple and blissful childhood, where we'd roam free till our hearts were content. No one locked their doors back then in my home village of Pomeroy, because no one ever had to.

Chapter Two

Early Memories

School days were spent at St Mary's Primary School in Pomeroy. While I can't say I learned that much, I definitely did enjoy those young and innocent days. Miss Keogh was my first teacher there when I started in 1947 at the age of five.

At school, we'd recite our 'times tables' until we knew them off by heart. We would all hope to be picked to clean the blackboard or, better again, to do 'roll call', because that meant we could put a hand on the answer book behind the teacher's back and cheat our way through the tests set for that day!

I was good at essay writing, called 'compositions' back then, but I was a disaster when it came to maths. In the eleven-plus exam, I remember drawing a square and putting the signs for a half and a quarter in it, and not knowing what on earth I was doing. And when it came to long division, I had not a clue! Needless to say, I didn't pass the eleven-plus!

There was an open fire in school. We used to get wee bottles of milk, which we'd carry in a crate to the front of the fireplace to let them warm. There was always a rush to get the warmest one. There were just two class-rooms in the school – one for infants and another for children up to fifteen years old. We went home for lunch every day, which was usually some 'bread boily', and we were always very well looked after and warm in a happy and peaceful home.

Josie McKernan was my best friend throughout my school days. One day, as a dare, she climbed out through the window and walked around the

A night out with my cousin Celine and my best friend from school Josie McKernan.

school to the front door to get back in. There were a few of us standing with our backsides to the door, not letting her in. When it finally opened, though, we were well caught out, as it was in fact the teacher, Miss Devlin, and she wasn't a bit impressed with our antics! Josie was an amazing handball player. She and I had many a day's fun filled with laughter and adventures, for which I will always remember her.

Miss Devlin, who taught me from the age of eight, was small in stature. She used to stand by the fire, warming herself until her legs would be roasting. She didn't push us too much, but she was a lovely and warm person. We all did what we had to do and no more, but we did what we were told and were taught manners.

The lads would salute the priests as a sign of respect and if we did something wrong, we'd soon get a slap. But even that didn't really stop us from making the same mistakes over and over again! Then the cane came into use in the early 1950s, and it was a mighty weapon. I remember it being very nippy. After a few taps of the cane, we never objected to the discipline and we definitely didn't make the same mistakes again!

I made my first communion in Pomeroy. I had two dresses which I wore at the same time, because one had holes in it and the other covered them up. My sister Mary wore a fancy blue feathery thing in her hair, and I wore the same veil that my ancestors wore, which I'm told was a hundred years old. For my confirmation, I chose the name Maeve, which was suggested to me by a close family friend, Mary-Jane Lagan. She told me it was the name of the first Irish queen, so maybe my notions of being a queen started a lot earlier than I thought!

During our breaks at school, we would play hopscotch and skipping in the schoolyard, and on 1 May every year, we loved to go around the houses and throw flowers on the doorsteps to celebrate May Day.

We often went to Margaret Trainor's ice cream shop on the way home from school for a dish of ice cream. Margaret lived above the shop, and when she would go up the stairs, Josie would stand on duty while I put my hand into the big tub and got us some extra scoops!

Our clothes were usually hand-me-downs, though we would get the odd item from the stalls from time to time, which was a real treat. One December, I wrote to Santa, or 'Santy' as he was known in our house, for a doll's pram, and I thought he got mixed up because it went next door to Olive Devlin's house instead! The walls between our houses were so thin that we'd be able to shout back and forth to each other, asking what each of us got from Santy. The Devlins often visited us on Christmas Day. Despite his tendency to make the odd wee mistake, I believed in Santa wholeheartedly until I was fourteen. My favourite present ever was a red balloon, which didn't last long as it bumped off the range in the kitchen on Christmas Night and went out with a bang! Most years, I'd get a ragdoll, some chocolate and an apple and an orange in my stocking, so I always did well, even if I never did get that pram that went next door.

Our days after school were spent playing and making up our own fun, whatever came our way. When Fulton's goat died next door to us, about six of us wrapped it up and carried it on our shoulders to the fields, where we buried it and put a cross and flowers on its grave and even had a funeral for it. We snuck in the odd smoke from time to time; I was the supplier, and would hide them in the elastic legs of my knickers! We puffed in Major Alexander's hay shed at Pomeroy Forest, where he owned an estate. We spent a lot of time there, climbing up and sliding down the hay

Pomeroy had, and still has, a massive sporting community for Gaelic

At school in St Mary's, Pomeroy in 1947. I'm in the back row, fourth from the right.

Games. My family all loved to get involved, with my father playing many roles on the local committee down the years. I played camogie, and would sometimes play for the neighbouring village, known as 'The Rock'. But when they made me goalie and I let thirteen goals in, my sporting career was finished. They never asked me back again!

My interest in music was beginning to show at this age. My cousins, the Quinn girls, and I would hold our very own concerts at the weekends, at the barn loft in Gortnagarn. We'd sing songs and pretend that we were on stage. We'd put up a sign stating our entry fee of one penny, and I don't think we ever had more than one customer. Our intentions to entertain were obvious, though about as successful as my sporting attempts!

* * *

Daddy bought a shop in the town when I was nine years old, which gave us all plenty of jobs to get on with. It really was at the heart of the community, so we got to see and hear all of the comings and goings. I was an expert by the grand old age of nine at weighing stuff, having helped my Granda out so often. It just became a way of life for us, and we all enjoyed every minute of it. The shop was next door to the parochial house where the priest lived. Ours was the only shop with a phone, so many people came into the shop to use it. We'd often take calls for local farmers, or they'd call in to ring the bull man, if he was needed. But sometimes they'd forget what they came in for, as they'd be too busy chatting and there'd be trouble on the farm when they left it too late. We took calls for the priest too, when he was away, so we'd be dealing with all sorts of matters, and no two days were the same.

When Daddy bought the shop, we moved from the 'top o' the town' to a house on The Diamond. That house was known as a 'céilí house', where there was always a lot of football talk and the sounds of laughter. My sister Margaret and I shared a bed together, and it was very soft, so in later years when I would come in late at night from singing at the dances, I would sink right into the middle and poor Margaret would feel my freezing cold feet on her back. Or I'd come in with a migraine or feeling sick and would wake her up, God love her! The house was often packed in the evenings, and you couldn't see your finger in front of you for smoke, between the cigarettes and the kitchen range they were all gathered around. We used to sit on the stairs and listen to the locals telling yarns and stories about banshees till the fire went out. Some of the women in the company would be afraid to go home when it all got too much for them!

When an old neighbour was dying, a few of the local men were sitting, waiting for her to pass, when an unmerciful wailing sound came from out-side. All of the big brave men were convinced it was a banshee and the final sign of her imminent death, but they obviously had been telling – and believing – too many ghost stories, for she went on to live for another year. Later, they copped on that the noise had only been a dog outside howling into the night!

My father loved giving us extra little jobs to do as we got older, and one of those was to help out in the bog with cutting the turf. But on one occasion, my brother Plunkett and I didn't exactly get the instructions right and we ended up in a bit of bother. 'Foot the turf,' we'd been told by Daddy before we left. What he meant was to stack the turf up into little criss-crossed bundles. We had never heard the term before, and didn't think to ask what he meant. Anyway, off we set, and when we got there, Plunkett turned to me and said:

'What are we meant to be doing?'

'Daddy said to foot the turf,' I replied, 'so surely that means we put our foot to it?'

And that's exactly what we did. We kicked the turf with our feet, and any stacks that were built, we kicked those down too. We got home that evening, delighted with our day's work, and as we sat at the dinner table, Daddy was all pleased when we told him we'd footed all the turf like he asked us to. Of course, when he got there and saw the mess we had made, we were sent right back up to the bog to fix all our damage. Imagine how simple we thought our job was, only to find it to be as sophisticated as making stacks. Not so easy with so many broken bits after all our kicking!

Daddy had a strong personality and he was definitely the boss in our house.

'Look after the children till I get home, Josie,' was a regular saying to my mother and off he'd set on his horse-drawn bread van, singing to himself as he did his rounds. He was a fine singer, and a talented songwriter too, and when the electric would go out at home, he'd gather us all around the fire and we'd sing songs together. 'My Mother's Rosary' was one of his favourites.

Daddy's bread run meant he always had an early start. Sometimes the visitors who came 'on their céilí' to our house would overstay, and he would

The Big Snow in Pomeroy in 1947. My father stands beside the horse-drawn bread van (second from the right), and with him are (l–r) my uncle Peter, our next-door neighbour Tommy Devlin, and Packie Murphy.

find it hard to stay up too late. One night, it all became a bit much. The boys were still debating and talking outside the front door and keeping everyone awake, so he reached out the window and poured a cup of water down over their heads. Of course the lads, who were mostly neighbours visiting after their committee meeting, thought that the water was something less favourable, so they took Daddy's wheelbarrow and put it away up high at the nearby Hibernian hall. They came back to the house and posted a note which said:

If you look down the street to the AOH hall,
You'll see there a barrow high up on the wall.
Just think of the boys who were standing below,
When you emptied the piss pot all over the show!

There was always lots of carrying on like that around our house. But, no matter what they argued about, or how bad the argument got, they still all came back for more the next night. The committee would meet in the local hall and then finish off their meeting in our house, where they'd eat 'fruit dishes' (ice cream and strawberries with lemonade) or 'sliders' (ice cream with wafers) and they'd talk and debate and argue about football for hours on end. Mammy enjoyed it, and she'd make the tea or else sit and knit as the conversation went on around her.

We had a big range in the kitchen and we'd wrap the lids in tea-towels to make our own type of hot water bottles. We all loved baking. One day my sister Angela made a lovely apple tart, of which she was very proud. She gave a slice to a local man, Harry McFlynn, and when poor old Harry died later that day, Angela was convinced that she'd poisoned him!

At the age of eleven, I was a bit of a wanderer, and I went to Sligo with a couple called Frank and Mary-Jane Lagan, who owned a pub there. Frank and Mary-Jane had adopted a little girl called Marie, and I was sent to look after her. The child was about three years old. I remember bringing her for a walk one day by the river and she fell in, and two local girls, Maisie McDaniels and her sister Deirdre, had to pull her out! I stayed with the family for a few weeks, but when I rang Pomeroy and heard Daddy's voice, I realised I wasn't as smart as I thought I was. The homesickness I felt was overwhelming.

I can still see Mammy when I got home, wearing a green smock with big black dots. Later, she fetched herself a basin and a big jug, and we were all sent to bed. During the night, Daddy woke us up and told us we had a new baby brother, and he was to be called Kieran. Even at the age of eleven, I had no idea what was happening until the child was born, but I was glad to be back in Pomeroy nonetheless, and delighted with my new baby brother. I really did help to rear Kieran, and I loved pushing him in the pram around Pomeroy. I remember one day, he fell off the chair and hurt himself, and I think I cried more with worry than he did from being hurt!

We lost our Granda Bigley about a year after Kieran was born, which was a big shock as he was only fifty-five years old. Granda had done a country run into the more secluded parts of our community, delivering bits from his shop, and one night he couldn't find the wee book he kept all his records in. He searched the house for it and still couldn't find it, and the stress of it brought on a heart attack, which he never recovered from.

I remember Mammy and Daddy coming home after hearing the news at Granny's. Kieran had climbed out of his cot, and was standing on his own at the top of the stairs. It was a miracle they came in when they did and that he didn't fall. We were all taken up to see Granda and say our good-byes. Looking back, I don't think we realised how young he was, but it was sudden and such a loss to our family.

After Granda's passing, our Granny Bigley depended a lot on us. We would all help out as much as we could, in and around our school commitments, so she could keep things going around the shop.

For most of us children, our school days finished at the age of fifteen, unless your parents chose to pay you into a secondary school. That certainly wasn't for me, so I set out to get a job. I can't say I was ever very academic, so I was happy enough to leave my days of education and go out into the big, bad world of earning a living. I left school on a Friday and started work on the Monday in the I.J. Fisher & Co. Hat Factory in Cookstown. Little did I know that a whole new career in a very different world was just around the corner.

Chapter Three

Factory Girl

I was only a child really when I started my 'grown-up' working life on a morning in June 1957 at the age of fifteen. I had a couple of days to get ready after finishing school on the Friday. I'll never forget my first day. I wore a skirt and blouse which had come from America, and a pair of kitten-heeled shoes. I was already far from my comfort zone – I'd much rather have been paddling in the river than wearing such grown-up clothes! Going to Fisher's Hat Factory was like going to America itself. Apart from my stint in Sligo a few years before, I had never really been far from home and the people I loved.

I got the bus at 7.30am and clocked in, and was put into the main shop, which was where they started making the hats. All I knew was that the hats were made from rabbit fur. I wasn't sure if they were Irish rabbits or rabbits from other countries, but we made a lot of hats and there was a lot of water involved! We had to stand for most of the day, putting the beginnings of what would become a hat into a huge multi-roller, which was a bit like a mangle. The hats would move on through many different stages before ending up at the clipping department, where the finished piece was made. They were men's hats and were exported all over the world by I.J. Fisher & Co.

Because of all the water around us, we had to stand on duckboards. My feet would be blistered sore from contact with the water for so long in my wee kitten heels, which were too tight anyway – I am nearly sure they belonged to our Annette, so it's no wonder they didn't fit!

After I moved to the clipping department, I sat beside Maisie Morton from Cookstown, and the two of us became close friends. My sister Angela and some of my cousins worked there too, but they didn't stay as long on the job as I did. I really loved working in Fisher's, and when I did leave to work in Woolworth's in Dungannon, I only spent seven months there before I went back to Fisher's again.

With my work colleagues in Woolworth's, Dungannon, second from the right.

The girls I worked with would sing away at the tops of their voices, and I'd be one of the main culprits, singing song after song over the noise of the machines. These were some of the happiest times of my life, at work in that factory. Every day, I'd bring in a few slices of bread for my lunch. I'd eat Marie biscuits between my bread with a cup of tea in the canteen. Work started at 8am and didn't finish until six in the evening. When I started, I earned £3 and ten shillings, which didn't get me too far! I gave the £3 to my father and kept the ten shillings for the bus fare for the week.

There was still time for fun, though. While Elvis stormed the charts at the height of his career, we Tyrone girls were more interested in the Clarie Hayden Roadshow, a home-made family variety show that travelled through towns and villages, entertaining the locals. Clarie himself was a comedian, and his family were all very popular entertainers. They'd erect a large tent in Pomeroy and take over the local hall. They'd stay for a week, hosting very popular talent competitions – our own version of 'The X Factor' back then! Mary McConnell and I were invited to the Roadshow to do our party piece. We sang Brahms' 'Lullaby', and scooped the first prize, which earned us a grand five shillings between us, or half a crown each. It was only for a laugh and none of us took our win very seriously but I was secretly delighted. It was the first time I'd won anything since my confirmation day, when I'd got a shilling for catching a duck at the circus! Maybe the experience of hosting concerts at Harte's Yard for one penny was beginning to pay off!

The Clarie Hayden Roadshow, like the circus, would move on, but our evenings were then filled with céilís and craic that we didn't have to travel far to get to. Pomeroy Hall was a regular host to the very popular Old Cross Céilí Band, and I went one night with my best friend Josie, my cousin

Celine and a crowd of friends from my old school days. We danced the Waves of Tory, the Sweets of May, a High Cauled Cap and two-hand reels – all well-known traditional Irish dances – and the sweat would be lashing off us as we hopped and skipped and laughed around the hall. I was a good enough dancer, I suppose, and I won a couple of medals at the feis, but I was no Michael Flatley!

In fact, when it came to taking part in anything musical, I must have been like an Ever Ready battery, because when John O'Neill from the Old Cross Céilí Band called for someone to join them for a song that night in 1962 – just like they always did – Josie and the girls dared me to go up. I sang 'Wolfe Tone's Grave' while the other girls danced along.

The Old Cross Céilí Band had been on the road for a few years by then. The next evening, when I came home from work in the factory, John O'Neill and Mickey McNally from the Old Cross were at my house. They had a proposal for me.

Margaret McKearney, who sang during the breaks at the céilís, had taken ill, and they needed a stand-in. Even though I was still working in Fisher's, I rose to the challenge and, on 11 May in Ardboe Hall, I made my official debut. My singing career, little did I know, had just begun. I was the modern-day equivalent of a support act, only instead of singing *before* the main act as a support act normally would, I'd go on stage during their break and sing a few songs while they had a well-earned cup of tea. I was delighted to be asked to do this, and was certainly up for the challenge, but their invitation had come as a big surprise.

Soon, I was on the road, travelling to céilís and parish halls with the band – Brian McNally on bass, Tom Quinn on accordion and banjo, Pat Hamill on fiddle, John O'Neill on accordion, Brian Coyle on drums (later replaced by Kevin Casey) and Mickey McNally on guitar. The men all wore white shirts and dicky bows, and I wore a white dress with a petticoat and red cummerbund, thinking I was very special indeed!

The céilís back then would go on for hours and hours, so when the boys in the band needed some time out, it was over to me to entertain the crowds. I'd sing half-a-dozen songs, which could be nothing faster than a quickstep according to Irish tradition in the halls across the country. So strict were the Roman Catholic priests who ran the céilís, we were too afraid to step out of the box and sing anything more exotic, for fear of being excommunicated! There were strict rules in the halls, all enforced by the religious organisers. They insisted on no alcohol (they were widely known as 'dry halls'), and an appropriate distance between men and women dancing. In fact, the men would stay at one side of the hall and the women at the other and the priests would patrol the place, making sure that no one got too close or personal!

I was very nervous my first time performing with the Old Cross, at Ardboe that night in May 1962. It's a date now etched in my mind as the beginning of a whole new life and a whirlwind career in music. Of course, I had no idea that night when I took the mic and sang. But I soon got the hang of it. I also earned ten shillings a show – the same as I was getting for my week's work in Fisher's after I paid my housekeeping, and even that was used for bus fare. I didn't know myself, having some extra money to actually spend as I pleased, and I began to save the odd wee bit here and there.

We were out many nights of the week. Even though I was twenty years old, I still felt about ten years of age, because in the early 1960s, we had to ask our parents' permission to do anything or go anywhere. We daren't come home too late, no matter what our excuse. There was a stair in our house that creaked, and if my father heard us step on it, he'd check the time that we'd returned.

'Who's that?' he'd shout from his bedroom.

'It's me,' I'd reply every time, knowing what was coming next.

'What time of the night is it?' I would always trim back an hour or two, which let me off many times. I soon learned to avoid that creaky step.

Looking back now, asking permission to come and go at twenty years of age might seem unbelievable, but we lived in very different times. We respected the rules of the house, whether we liked them or not. I admired my father for keeping an eye on us all, which I'm now sure wasn't easy with such a big family to care for.

I remember Daddy going through each and every one of our names at night until he knew where everyone was.

'Where's Margaret?' he asked one night. She was out a bit later than she should have been and, being one of the youngest in the house, Daddy began to panic.

Angela arrived home, but still no Margaret. I arrived home, and still no Margaret. Daddy was becoming very cross. When she did eventually get back, I had to hide her in the bedroom and pretend that she had been there for a while. Daddy felt bad for being so cross with us all, and he took me downstairs for a bun and a bottle of Lucozade. He was a big softie behind it all, but we knew our boundaries and we always had respect for him.

Plunkett was locked out one night when he arrived home very late, and he was contemplating sleeping in the byre. When he looked around, there was Angela standing at the byre door, facing the same problem. All they could do was laugh.

By now my social and working lives were mixed together as one, with the Old Cross Céilí Band becoming more and more busy. Late nights and early starts became normal for me as, much to my surprise, I adapted to being a singer by night and a factory girl by day.

Chapter Four

The Old Cross Céilí Band

Margaret McKearney never did come back to the Old Cross Céilí Band, so I was soon a permanent part of their show. We performed at carnivals, as well as céilís and barn dances across the country. The carnivals were a lot of fun and were a sign of how, at the time, festivals could be pulled together on very small budgets. Basically, a village or a community would set up a marquee in a field, and would host music and entertainment over a period of up to two weeks at a time. So there was always plenty of work for our band locally. We'd dress up in fancy costumes to add more colour to our act, which always went down a treat.

Looking back, I never did really think very much about my transition from factory girl to singer – it just seemed to happen naturally. Although

I was still working long hours in the factory every day, I was also now seen as a 'real' singer. And, having grown up with my father singing around the house all the time, and everywhere the sounds of the accordion band that my siblings played in, music was something I took to very naturally. I just went with the flow as the demands of the Old Cross Céilí Band became more and more frequent.

As much as I was taking it all in my stride, I clearly recall the second night I performed with the Old Cross, which was at Forkhill Carnival. That night, I lost my nerve on stage and forgot the words. I froze, and didn't know what to do, but thankfully Gerry Burns of the Jackie Hurst Céilí Band – also on the bill that night – came up on stage to help me. I'll never forget him for it. It was an awful experience altogether, but I later learned that these things happen and the show must go on! Over the years, I learned to deal with moments like that. Now, when I forget the words, I just make it part of my show and I don't think anyone bats an eyelid. But back then, as a young girl starting out, it was a truly terrifying experience. I suppose you could call it my first encounter with stage fright!

Apart from that wee blip at Forkhill, life on the road with the band was always positive, and I got to see many places and faces along the way. I suppose my wandering feet and sense of wonder had never really left me. I loved getting out and about, even if I was exhausted the next morning, facing into my day's work at the factory.

I was absolutely in my element in those days. My life was very busy, and always exciting. The band travelled together in an estate car. Pulling a small trailer behind it that we called the Old Bull Cart, off we'd set to venues near and far, dressed to the nines. I wore big flouncy dresses, with petticoats, in all different colours. One of my favourites was an orange dress I wore

Me with a short hairstyle in the 1960s.

as bridesmaid at the wedding of our bandmate Pat Hamill and his wife Teresa. I got plenty of wear out of it after the wedding, that was for sure, as it made a perfect outfit for the stage!

While we were all reared on Irish folk and traditional céilí music, Mickey McNally of the Old Cross had a fine collection of country music. One day, he gave me a Hank Williams record to listen to. The song was called 'My Son Calls Another Man Daddy', and I was instantly hooked. Soon I was listening to Kitty Wells and Patsy Cline, and dying to sing some country music on stage.

Teresa Rafferty owned a shop in Pomeroy and she used to order in the country records for me. I'd devour them with excitement at discovering all these new stars; I loved them all, but my absolute favourite was George Jones.

The lads in the band were keen to play country too, but anything we liked we had to convert into old-time waltzes, because the Catholic clergy prohibited us from bringing anything new into our traditional Irish sets. In those days, you would have been excommunicated if you broke the rules in the céilí halls so we didn't dare upset anyone. We knew the Church's rules were not to be broken!

So it was the parish carnivals, rather than the céilí halls, that became our testing ground for these new country sounds and, because they ran for two weeks at a time between April and September, we had plenty of work around Tyrone and near home.

The carnival scene gave us a little bit of freedom in the music we could try out. The showband era was in its heyday with bands like the Clipper Carlton, the Royal Showband, the Dixies and hundreds more travelling up and down the country, and there was a new desire in young people to get up and dance. The performers, too, were standing up, rather than sitting on chairs like the céilí bands did, so we tweaked our set and our style and for a while we became the Old Cross Bandshow in order to move with the times. The change in our name was a difficult one to communicate, but we persisted when taking bookings to ensure the new name stuck. We used the phrase 'formerly known as the Old Cross Céilí Band' to ensure followers knew it was us!

Our next step as a band was to record a song, and we headed off to Billy McBurney's Outlet Studios in Belfast to lay down two: 'Come, Me Little Son' and 'Old Ardboe' (the B-side). We sent the record off to radio stations. At that time, a wee backhander worked well to ensure we got some airtime, but a verse and chorus was all we managed to have played on Radio Éireann (renamed Radio Telefís Éireann or RTÉ in 1966). We were very disappointed that they didn't play the whole song. It was very hard to get a song played by the national stations. Our only hope of airtime was on pirate radio shows, which filled the airwaves with bands like us: bands who hadn't hit the charts and never dreamed they would.

* * *

Country music, or, as it soon became known in Ireland, country and western, was one of the greatest and earliest influences on the showband era, and that is where we really wanted to be – using those American sounds we were hearing on Mickey's record collection and the music I was gathering from Teresa Rafferty's shop. But, unlike the American country music we were listening to, our versions of these songs were designed for just one dance style: jiving, a mainstay of dancehalls in Ireland throughout the 1960s. One day, Mickey McNally had a brainwave. He knew we were itching to test this new sound live, so he suggested we change the name of the band to reflect the change in our music and the direction we want to take the band. We had the perfect mix of the céilí band style, showband rock'n'roll and a big chunk of that American country sound thrown in for good measure, and it seemed to come naturally to us. As we were driving past Parkanaur Forest, just outside Dungannon, one of the lads said:

'I think we need something with a country flavour to it.'

And so we had our name, the Country Flavour, and a new era of singing the music of my heart was born.

Soon, the bookings for the Country Flavour were coming in thick and fast. We found ourselves a manager in Nelius O'Connell, one of the greatest promoters of his era, who took us the length and breadth of Ireland. We even got a pay rise! When we'd play venues in big cities like Galway, at least four hours from Pomeroy, I'd have to rush home from work in the afternoon, get ready and then hit the road with the band, and later, drive through the night to make it back just in time to catch the bus to work at

8am. The bus driver, Packie Hurson, would be standing by, knowing the score and how hungry I would be, and he'd wait until I grabbed a few slices of bread to eat before he headed for Cookstown. He was a lifesaver, as I'd have been docked pay if I was late to the factory floor. At night, I'd change out of my factory clothes and put on my stage outfits, which I absolutely loved – I thought I was the bee's knees in my wee miniskirts in navy or red, with fringes on them that I had sewn on myself. I would top off the look with a waistcoat and white boots, and in no time I was good to go. With all the coming and going, I soon figured out how to make use of my daytime breaks, by having a wee snooze under the coats when the time was right!

The Old Cross Céilí Band, Carrickmore, Country Cavan, early 1960s.

By 1964, after seven years working in the factory, I knew it was time to move on. We were becoming more busy and recognised for our work, and venues in England were beginning to book us. We found ourselves especially busy during Lent, when no entertainment was allowed in Ireland. Again, this was a rule enforced by the Catholic Church, which insisted that dancing during Lent was inappropriate. Needless to say, we went elsewhere to keep the band busy. So, I made the big decision to leave the factory and focus on my music career, but this couldn't be done without my father's permission.

I was so nervous that it took me a full week to tell him – or ask him, rather – but I needn't have worried, for my father understood. He gave me his blessing, knowing that we were on the road to success. He also knew and trusted the boys in the band, who looked after me very well. Besides, there was one band member who had already caught my eye more than the others. So I knew, just as my father did, that everything was going to work out just fine.

'Come, Me Little Son' was released by Dolphin Records in 1968, under the famous Jim Aiken (who went on to create Aiken Promotions). One night, in the Starlight Ballroom in Belfast, the County Tyrone singer Eileen Donaghy presented me with a copy of our very first record in a wooden frame. Eileen was an international star at the time, and it was like getting a gold disc! It really was a big deal to me, and I still treasure it, even though it's a bit dusty now!

We were now a fully-fledged country and western band. The social scene in Ireland was changing, and for me, my personal life was set to change too.

Chapter Five

The Country Flavour

I knew Tom Quinn from a very early age; he was from the neighbouring village of Galbally. I'd seen him at football matches, and I had my eye on him, you could say, since I joined the band in 1962. In those days, having a 'wee notion' on someone was very innocent.

When I joined the Old Cross Céilí Band, Tom played the accordion, piano, banjo and mandolin. Throughout those years, from venue to venue, we often sat together in the back of the van. It was a very platonic friendship, which slowly developed into something else. Looking back, we were probably an item much longer than we even realised it.

In the 1970s, the country music radio scene was still very difficult to crack, but the popularity of the Country Flavour grew with support from

Me and Tom in our younger days.

the pirate stations like Radio Erneside, and by 1971, we began to attract big crowds who would stand and watch us as well as dance. One of those who watched us on many occasions, particularly in the Glenfarne Ballroom of Romance, was a young teenager called Dan O'Hara. He was like a Teddy Boy in his black, three-quarter-length jacket with a velvet collar and his long, black hair. He was a huge country music fan, and he played lead guitar. He had just the right sound, and the knowledge of the country and jive scene that we needed, and so we invited him to join the band. 'Dano', as he was known, became an essential part of the band, and the Country Flavour enjoyed a new lease of life after his arrival.

Dano came from Blacklion in Cavan, but moved to Pomeroy when he joined the band, lodging with a lady called Mrs McGuckin. I used to joke with him that he was so skinny, he'd fit through the eye of a needle! He was a real character and a lovely lad. I remember him coming up to our home place. He'd take the spuds out of the saucepan and put them on the range, still in their skins, and he'd nibble at them when they got nice and crispy. He soon moved in next door to us in The Diamond, and he never left our house.

'Jaysis, Josie, I've two boiled eggs on!' he said one day in a panic, realising that the potato skins had distracted him from his own cooking next door. He raced out the door, and when he got there the boiled eggs had exploded all over his kitchen!

Dano was one of the best guitar players around, and he was soon known as 'King of the Strings'. He became highly respected throughout Ireland as the years went by, so I'm very proud that we invited him to be a part of the Country Flavour in his youth. Declan Nerney even recorded a song about him, called 'My Hero Lies in Cookstown' (written by Henry McMahon), which is a testament to just how well considered he would become by some of country's most popular singers.

As Ireland's love of country music grew, so did our popularity, and I was beginning to be recognised when I was out and about, in the shops, on the streets and even at funerals! Among our fellow musicians, the band became known as Philomena Begley and the Country Flavour, and things really began to take off. John Fitzsimons took over from Neilus as our manager, and in 1972, we made our first full album, *Truck Drivin' Woman*. We'd already released a few singles and EPs in the 1960s, including 'The Box That It Came In' in 1968. The album was released by Mick Clerkin, owner of Release Records in Dublin.

When we would travel into towns – Granard, County Longford, stands out – dozens of children would run alongside the van, looking for 'snap snaps', as they called them, of the band. And fans began to gather at the dance halls, in advance, waiting for us to arrive. Our schedules became so hectic that we sometimes had to stop the milkmen on the road for a drink when we hadn't had time to eat on the road. There were no twenty-four-hour shops back then!

Country music in Ireland in the early 1970s was really booming. We got to perform alongside many other acts including Hugo Duncan and the Tall Men, Brian Coll and the Buckaroos, Big Tom, Larry Cunningham, and Eileen Reid and the Cadets, who used to drive around in Vauxhall Cadet cars. A pop band called the Memories brought a new element to the music scene. People also wanted new sounds, including rock'n'roll, and we catered to their tastes by adding some rock'n'roll numbers to our set.

* * *

In 1969, my father had built Pomeroy Hall (later known as Begley's Hall), with the vision of hosting community events, concerts and dances. Boy, it really made a difference to the life of our village, bringing many, many big names our way. My father decided to invest his own money into it. I helped him, contributing my savings book and its contents – I'd saved a bit of money by then, playing with the Country Flavour. After seven years in the music scene, I was in a much better position to help my parents out than I was before. I gave my mother a fiver every week towards housekeeping, a good bit of money back then, and I think I'd saved about £600, which really helped with the building costs.

Begley's Hall was a great success from the start, and I was delighted to take part in the official opening with the Country Flavour. Hundreds of people turned up that night, and it was probably one of the largest social events ever to have been hosted in Pomeroy. From then on, Friday night dances were held at the hall, with my brother Patsy in charge of booking the bands. Locals were treated to performances by the Indians, Hootenany, the Venturers, Roly Daniels, Gene Stuart, Brian Coll and many more major players from all over the country. Bands loved coming to Pomeroy, because they were well fed with Mammy's famous apple tarts back at our house after the show. She would have the tarts lined up on the range, piping hot, just out of the oven. Musicians would put their arms around them, pretending to be afraid of someone stealing them. I suppose it was a very nice touch to get such hospitality after an evening entertaining.

One summer's night in the early 1970s, the Indians had just performed to a large crowd and packed up their van. They were about to call over to our home place for a drop of tea when gunfire, like a really loud rat-a-tat-a-tat, broke out down at the local barracks. The band ducked for cover. It was the last thing anyone expected. The Troubles in the North had begun to brew by then, and Pomeroy police station was nearby, so we all knew that something was going on. The Indians were surprised and scared stiff. I can still see them today, falling to the ground and crawling across the street on their hands and knees until they reached the front door of our house. They were very glad of the safety of our house, and I bet apple tart never tasted as good as it did that night! But that was the way of our world back then, and the gunfire was rarely mentioned again.

Bingo was popular in Begley's Hall as well. I recall one evening in particular when it was so packed that the buses outside were still full of people who couldn't fit into the hall, so my brother Kieran set up a loudspeaker system outside and they played their bingo on the buses.

When discos took over from live music dances many years later, the hall became less popular and sadly began to fail. But the chip van that had been parked outside the hall every week still turned up regardless. Kieran often wondered how it was worth their while when the footfall just wasn't the same, but when he asked the man in the chip van, the man said:

'The crowds round here might not be as big anymore, but those who do come here are still a big eating crowd.'

The Country Flavour, c.1967.

The Country Flavour had brought a uniqueness to the Irish sound – a genre, even. Together with a few co-lovers of Irish country, we carried our banner throughout Ireland and England, slowly breaking down barriers and winning over audiences. Our sound was truly groundbreaking at the time, and I think we were certainly pioneers of country music in England, having done much of the spadework that laid foundations for what is now a massive country scene all over Europe. The popularity of country music in Ireland, especially in the North, showed no signs of slowing down either. The Country Flavour were busy playing six nights a week.

* * *

The Country Flavour years brought me some amazing international experiences and opportunities. We travelled to America in 1972, playing in New York, Boston, Philadelphia and Chicago as guests of an Irish-American called Bill Hardigan. He owned a venue called the Tower View and he arranged for us to play there, the Red Mill and the Jaeger House. Audience members gave us dollar notes to show their appreciation! I remember getting on a bus on my own in New York one day, and an Irish lady called Kathleen Tracey sat beside me. It turned out she was from Greencastle, just up the road from Pomeroy. Little did I know our paths would cross again when my only son would go on to marry her niece! It just shows how small the world is, and how you should really be nice to everyone you meet along the way, as you never know when or where you might meet again. This is even true in a city as huge as New York.

It was a real novelty to visit America, and we didn't need drink to have fun; life on the road brought many adventures anyway. We were all staunch Pioneers back then. I came from a Pioneer family, so I never really knew any other way of life, and there was never any temptation to have an alcoholic drink. With the characters who travelled with us, we always had plenty of antics going on and lots to talk about. Mickey McNally (a man with the same name as the Mickey in our band) was our roadie by night and a Pomeroy milkman by day, and he was always full of joy. Once we were playing Bellaghy Carnival, and while we were on stage, Mickey the Roadie was held up at gunpoint and the armed robbers demanded money from him. He came into the hall afterwards, waving his hands to let us know what had happened, but he was proud of the fact that they didn't get all of the money – in fact, they got very little. He had it well hid in the van, and the whole episode seemed more exciting than frightening to him.

One night, after playing in Cavan, we had all packed up and were ready to go. Tom and I headed off in one car, while the rest of the band followed us in the van ... or so we thought. We were just approaching Lisnaskea in Fermanagh when the police stopped us, and asked us had we noticed anyone missing. The guards from Cavan had contacted the police north of the border to tell them that someone had been left behind. Of course there were no mobile phones in those days, so we weren't able to call. We had to go all the way back to Cavan to solve the mystery. Sure enough, there was poor Mickey the Roadie, and he was hyperactive from all the drama. I had a tape recorder with me for learning songs and I recorded him telling his version of events:

'I went round the back to take a p*** and when I came back the van was away up the road like a f****n' swallow in summer!'

He just loved the fuss that came with having to contact the police and send out an SOS to be rescued. We laughed about that for many years to come!

On stage with the Country Flavour in Manchester in the early 1970s. Left to right: Tom Quinn, John O'Neill, me, Brian McNally, Kevin Casey, Pat Hamill, Dan O'Hara and Mickey McNally.

Back then, in the early 1970s, there were a lot of bands on the road, travel-ling from north to south and vice versa, and if we saw another van parked up on the side of the road, we'd often stop for a chat along the way. We took a packed lunch with us, even if we were only going an hour or two down the road, because we'd rarely have time to stop for long and have a proper meal. We soon got to know every 'gap in the hedge', and the best places to stop along each and every road. We really did become a family as we travelled together in those years, and all the while Tom and I were growing closer.

In 1969, Tom and I went to Monaghan, and there we got engaged, having managed to buy the ring just before the shops closed – a wee diamond with shoulders that cost forty-five Irish, pounds which were known as 'punts'.

Tom had been in the band before I started, of course, so I'd heard my sisters talk of him before I ever met him. In fact, I think he may have fancied them a little before he even noticed my existence! He used to play mandolin in McKeown's Céilí Band before the Old Cross came along, and a fine player he was, too. Our relationship was a platonic friendship at first, and not outwardly romantic – we weren't walking around hand-in-hand – but we had a deep connection and it proved to be something that just grew stronger and stronger. Tom was a quiet man then, sensible and steady, and I admired that in him. I still do to this day.

Five years later, on the night before our wedding, we played a gig at Pomeroy Hall. I had caught a very bad flu that was going around just a few days before the gig, but I got out of my sick bed that night to sing. Our big day was 2 February 1974, in the cathedral in Monaghan town, and I was thirty-two years old. On the morning of the wedding, I had some photos taken with my niece and godchild Louise Begley at the back door of my family home. My wedding ring was a lot cheaper than my engagement ring, at only £10, and I bought it myself in Dungannon. With my dress, I wore red-and-white polka-dot shoes, and a hat that was flung in the back of the car as soon as I left the house.

There were only seven people, including ourselves, at the ceremony, which was officiated by Fr Joe McVeigh. Our wedding party consisted of John Fitzsimons and his girlfriend, Ruth Brue, my sister Margaret and my youngest brother, Kieran. The excuse at the time for such a small gathering was that we were too busy for a big celebration, but the truth was I didn't want any fuss. We were married and went straight to the nearby Oriel Hotel for lunch, which cost £7 and 10 shillings in total. We received a few telegrams – one from Tony Loughman, head of Top Rank Entertainments in Castleblayney, and another from my brother Patsy. Then we headed off to Portumna in County Galway, where we were booked to play a gig that night. My sister Margaret phoned ahead to let the band know of our news, but their reaction was less than enthusiastic, which now I can totally understand.

We had been a band a very long time, and we really were like a family, so the boys were deeply disappointed that we hadn't told them our plans or invited them along to the ceremony. It was never our intention to offend anyone, but if we had begun to invite any more than those few who came along as witnesses, we wouldn't have known where to stop. There were just so many wonderful people in our lives. But on the day it was just how I wanted it – no commotion – and I still wouldn't change a thing. I have absolutely no regrets.

Meanwhile, because our wedding plans were really very swift, we hadn't had any time to prepare for our married life. But Tom's parents decided to move out of their farmhouse at The Mill in Galbally, having built a new bungalow, so we were able to move in and set up our first home as a married couple.

In Pomeroy, a few days after our wedding and our gig in Portumna, my sister Margaret had a box of household equipment and groceries ready for us to get us started. We set off to Tom's parents' house in Galbally where they were waiting for us with a big fire lit. It was my first time meeting them since Tom and I became a couple, and I was nervous of what they might think of me. I say this because back then women in show-business were often looked down upon. Some of my friends told me once to 'get a real job', and someone in our local shop had asked me, 'Are you the show-girl?' which didn't sound like a compliment. I took it all on the chin; I was enjoying my career to the full.

I do think it's funny how judgemental some people can be when they see a woman pursuing a career they don't consider 'the norm'. It's true that when I was younger, my main ambition was to be a nurse, but life led me down a very different path and my eyes were opened to a whole new world. Working at night, with an all-male band, singing about cheatin' husbands and divorce, was a far cry from the traditional nine-to-five and my very Catholic upbringing. I understand why some people, especially those in rural communities, would have found my choice strange. It's not to everyone's taste, but I had the support of my family and was having the absolute time of my life, so there's no way anyone, or any derogatory comment, would ever have stood in my way.

Tom's parents, much to my joy, were delighted to hear of our nuptials, and we moved into the house that night. The next day, we set off for a show in Glenfarne in County Leitrim. There was tension in the band for a while and, unfortunately, things didn't really improve from then. This made me sad but I suppose it was inevitable after a whole twelve years on the road together.

The following night we played in Newcastle West, County Limerick, then on to Dublin, then over to London to play the Royal Albert Hall with Larry Cunningham and Ray Lynam, in an all-Irish concert. When we got back, it was business as usual, but the vibe in the band was a bit low, as the post-wedding disquiet settled in like an elephant in the room.

So, the Country Flavour's time together came to a natural end shortly after Tom and I were married. I had to make one of the hardest decisions I ever had to make in this business, and we agreed to go our separate ways. It definitely wasn't a decision I took lightly, and I cried a lot – it was really like losing part of my family. We had come through so much, we had seen countless places and faces and had experienced many musical highs together, and to leave all that behind was a massive change for me. Thankfully, we have all stayed good friends. Never one to wallow, though, I was soon made an offer I couldn't refuse.

* * *

Tony Loughman, head of the promotion company Top Rank Entertainments and an up-and-coming manager from Castleblayney, had a vision for the country music scene in Ireland. I had taken part in a concert for him in Enniskillen, and he'd been watching the Country Flavour closely for over a year.

He had spotted the potential for what he called a country and western 'superband', with guitars, keyboards, accordions, drums, bass and brass. The works! Tony knew this superband would take the country music scene to a whole new level. His enthusiasm for, and his awareness of, what we and the Country Flavour had achieved so far was impressive, and his overall energy and ideas were contagious. On the phone that day, he asked Tom if he wanted to hear more. Of course he did!

Tony wanted to come and speak to Tom and me about it the next day. Just as promised, he arrived at our home with his wife, Joan, to make some initial suggestions about who he wanted to approach to be part of this new band. Who would play in the band, I wondered? Who would be the centre focus? What would we call the band? Who would be the singer? What exactly did Tony have in mind when he said 'superband'?

'Build a band around Philly herself,' said Tom and Tony's eyes widened. 'She's the big star. Let her front the new superband and you're guaranteed success.'

Tony (RIP) and Joan Loughman.

Tony was as excited about this idea as we were. It was time for a whole new challenge for Tom and me, and the chance to lead a new superband with a brass section and a big bold sound took my breath away. But where would we start?

Tony and Joan left our house that day with plenty on their minds. And we had plenty to figure out too. We were bursting with ideas ourselves, and had decided that a good name for the band would be something to do with some of my most popular songs. Later that afternoon, Tony and Joan arrived back to our house in Galbally, having travelled all the way from Castleblayney, with some mock posters saying Philomena Begley and Her Ramblin' Men. Well, it was perfect, and because Tony's commitment was seriously focused on making this work, we decided to go for it!

So we had found our name, and we knew what we needed. But where would we find our Ramblin' Men? They needed to be really at the top of their game if our superband was going to be as super as it sounded! Dano – a big part of the Country Flavour – decided to join us, and soon word got out that we were recruiting new members. There was a big buzz among a lot of Irish musicians who were keen to put their name in the hat.

Just a few days later, a car arrived onto our driveway, and out of it came the four men we had been hoping for. Kevin McGinty, Kevin Farley, Colm Keeley and Liam Gibson were keen to come on board to try out Tony's superband theory. We all knew immediately that these fellas were exactly what we were after, and they fitted the bill perfectly.

Philomena Begley and Her Ramblin' Men were ready to take the world by storm – but was the world ready for them? We would soon find out ...

Chapter Six

My Ramblin' Men

The original line-up of Philomena Begley and Her Ramblin' Men was Kevin Farley on brass and sax, Kevin McGinty on trumpet and bass, Colm Keeley on drums, Liam Gibson on rhythm guitar, Tom Quinn on keyboards, accordion and banjo, and Dan 'Dano' O'Hara on lead guitar. Some of them had commitments with Brian Coll to fulfil before we went on the road, so we had only one rehearsal before our first public appearance.

On Easter Sunday, 14 April 1974, I was booked to perform solo as a special guest at the Silk Cut Festival in London's Wembley Stadium, in front of 12,000 people. Ray Lynam and the Hillbillies played with me in an early matinee, and we left London that evening to make the Ramblin' Men's very first gig, back near home at the Four Seasons Hotel in Monaghan. All of this after only one rehearsal. Were we all mad in thinking this was going to actually work? Talk about being thrown in at the deep end! But Tony

Loughman was confident, and his excitement rubbed off on the rest of us. We were all keen to get stuck in.

Despite all the enthusiasm and excitement, as we travelled from England, I was as nervous as a kitten about what we were actually coming home to. Everyone had loved the Country Flavour, and were sad to see us break up (including me!), so what would they think of this new so-called superband of Ramblin' Men? I was afraid we might be arriving to an empty hall. What if Tony Loughman was wrong? What if we failed? My whole future career and reputation was set on the success of this new band and I had worked so hard for twelve years, carving out a name as a performing artiste, that I felt like I had a lot to lose should Tony's superband fall at the first hurdle.

Wembley with Ray Lynam had been such a thrill that day, but we weren't sure we could keep up the momentum for our Monaghan audience with an all-new look, feel and sound. Travelling from Dublin airport, I was still wearing the same frock I had on me on stage in London earlier that day. I had butterflies the whole way across the country. We were almost there, and would soon find out … it could go either way for us.

When we approached Monaghan, we were hit with a bit of a surprise. The traffic was bumper to bumper and I dreaded that as well as all the anxiety around how we would actually perform and what type of response we would get, now it looked like we were going to be late for our very first gig. The guards stopped our vehicle and told us there was an issue with crowd control.

'Crowd control?' we asked. 'Has something happened?'

'Nothing has happened, nothing bad anyway,' said the guard. 'There's a big new band in town and everyone is out to see them. Their name is Philomena Begley and Her Ramblin' Men.'

Left: With my siblings in our schooldays at St Mary's, Pomeroy.

Right: My sisters and I all dressed up. Left to right: Angela, Mary, Annette, Margaret and me.

Left: Helping out at the family farm.

Left: Tom on accordion during the Old Cross Céilí Band days.

Below: The Old Cross Céilí Band in our first ever promotional photo shoot, sometime around 1962!

Ready to sing in the swinging sixties.

Above: The Country Flavour.

Left: With my sister Margaret and my brother Kieran on our wedding day, in the cathedral in Monaghan, 1974.

Below: Me and my Ramblin' Men.

Above: With Joe Frazier, the time he visited Dundrum, County Down, in 1975.

Above: My brother Patsy Begley (RIP).

Below: Brian Coll and I enjoying the St Patrick's Day Parade in New York City, 1978.

Right: With Porter Wagoner in Nashville, 1978.

Below: Performing 'The Umbrella Song' at the International Country Music Festival at Wembley.

Right: My favourite blue suit, that I bought on my second visit to Nashville in October 1978.

Above: A press shot from the 1980s.

Below: With the late Glen Campbell in 1990. I was celebrating twenty-five years in the business, and Glen was celebrating twenty-one.

Above: At the Silkeborg Country Festival in Denmark with Shotgun, around 1990. Clockwise from top left: Patsy Tweedy, Seamus Rooney, Stephen Smith, myself and Liz Gordon.
Below: The end of a great night at the Central Ballroom in Newcastle, County Down.

Tom and I looked at each other. We couldn't believe it! The venue was packed to capacity, it seemed everyone really *had* come out to see the Ramblin' Men perform for the first time, and we were over the moon. Willie McKenna was taking the money on the door of the Four Seasons Hotel that night, and for years he took great pride in telling how he was there on the first night of the Ramblin' Men and that it was so packed they had to turn people away.

We didn't have fancy equipment or special effects like a lot of the bands use nowadays – we weren't used to monitors or those fancy yokes that create strobe lighting, and we had no big articulated lorries. The next evening after our debut, we performed on Easter Monday at Sixmilecross Carnival, and we received the same crowd all over again. This was the start of the big time for the Ramblin' Men. For a full year, we hardly got a night off at all.

Me and my Ramblin' Men. Clockwise from top left they are: Kevin McGinty, Tom Quinn, Kevin Farley, Dan O'Hara, Colm Keeley, Liam Gibson and me.

We took our on-stage appearance very seriously. The Ramblin' Men were dressed in specially made suits of pale blue or pink or royal blue or cream – all the colours of the rainbow, and all made to measure by Jas Fagan in Dublin.

Our first album was recorded at Castle Studios in Tony's hometown of Castleblayney, in the summer of 1975. The songs were sung by most members of the band. Dano and I sang 'Today, Tomorrow and Forever'; Dano sang 'Walking Piece of Heaven'; Colm sang 'Be My Guest'; Kevin Farley sang 'Laugh With Me, Sigh With Me'; and Kevin McGinty sang 'Hello Mary Lou'. Tom and Dano played an instrumental called 'The Wildwood Flower'. We recorded an excellent variety of songs for the album.

Tony was an astute manager, and his wife Joan was very involved in every aspect of the business, from the recording side of things to the live performances, as was Kevin Ward, who managed distribution for Top Rank. My new husband, Tom, took on the role of band leader. We had no big producers back then, and we just learned the songs and played them as it felt natural to. I picked my own songs, as did everyone else in the band. In our live gigs, we would throw in the odd chart hit to mix it up a bit, things like 'Devil Gate Drive' or 'Johnny B. Goode'. I did 'An American Trilogy', only recently made so famous by Elvis, which sounded first class with the brass in our band.

My Ramblin' Men and I got on like a house on fire. The band members were all good, honest, down-to-earth fellas, just like the Country Flavour boys before them, and once again, it was like being part of a big family.

Tom and I would travel together with Kevin Farley, while the others would go ahead in the van with all our PA equipment. Jimmy Lynch was our roadie then, and he was another real character. I can remember once, when we were playing in Wick in Scotland, the van broke down. While we were on stage, Jimmy dismantled the whole van engine, took it out piece by piece, and by the time the gig was over he had it all back in place and the van was going again!

But there was a night in winter in Letterkenny, many years later, when it was very cold and frosty and the antics were less jolly. Usually Jimmy would nearly have a speaker off the stage before the last song was finished, he was that eager to get organised and packed up, so we were surprised when we were all done that there was no sign of him. Tom went out to the van to look for him and found Jimmy lying at the wheel unconscious. He had been knocked out by the fumes from a stove he had lit in the back of the van to keep warm. One of the newer band members at the time, Hughie McKenna, was training to be a nurse, but even he couldn't get Jimmy to come round. We managed to get him to hospital, and he remained unconscious until the next morning. The medical staff told us that if he had been left for another ten minutes in the van, he would have been dead.

By the mid-1970s, our success was growing, but the Troubles, as they were known, were also peaking. Over the years, during certain flash points, my family hosted refugees from towns like Belfast and Derry where the streets were lined with fire, houses were being burned out and homes were being raided. These places were deemed unsafe, and many children were sent to counties along the North-South border, the 'border counties', where they could be away from bombs and bullets for weeks at a time.

Being on the road so much, there was always the fear of what could go very wrong. One night in Ballinderry, which straddles Derry and Tyrone, a group of masked men came onto the stage as we were performing and told the band to stop playing. I jumped off the stage and I swear I have never jumped so high in my life. These kinds of incidents were regularly in the news during the Troubles but it was still absolutely petrifying to experience it first-hand. Other threats were on our minds: particularly car bombs, because we were always on the road. Explosions and gun attacks had put an end to the carnivals in marquees. These venues were deemed simply too exposed to be safe. Other singers and groups from south of the border would be escorted into the North to perform, but we would just have to get on with it. And that's exactly what we did.

But one night in November 1974, the Troubles came home to my husband's family. We had played a gig in Ballymena in County Antrim, and had made it home safely that night. The next morning, though, we were woken by Tom's father knocking hard on our front door.

'Get up, Tom! Pat Falls was shot dead last night. Get up!'

Pat Falls was married to Tom's sister Maureen. He was an innocent man who had left a job in Birmingham to help with his brother's pub and shop at home. It was during a time of many tit-for-tat killings, when anyone could be called a target. His six children moved over to Galbally from Birmingham after his death, and they lived with Tom and me for a year. They were aged from thirteen to just six years old, and it was devastating to watch poor Maureen struggle on without her husband, and those children without their father. For me, it was one of the worst incidents of the Troubles, to witness such heartache and pain so close to home.

The killing of members of the Miami Showband in July 1975 added to our fears. We knew them all, of course, and it shook the music community considerably, as we all knew it could have been any of us murdered like that. Tom Dunphy, a singer with Brendan Bowyer, had been killed in a car accident two days before, so we were doubly shocked. The attack on the Miami Showband, on their way from Banbridge to Dublin, stopped a lot of bands in the country scene from touring in the North. A lot of the bands were too afraid to come anywhere near towns that had welcomed them so well in previous years. They were very sad and very frightening times, to say the least, but the likes of the Ramblin' Men, Brian Coll, Hugo Duncan, Brendan Quinn and Susan McCann kept playing. Yes, we were stopped at night on the roads at army checkpoints, but we were never threatened, and we always managed to keep our show on the road with none of us getting hurt, thank God.

The news in the 1970s was all 'bombs, bullets and barricades', and life in the north of Ireland shifted from peaceful, rural towns and villages to constant threats of death and injury on our doorstep. We merged into a world of 'extraordinary normality', as steel gates were erected in towns, control zones were designated and our handbags were searched entering shopping centres. It was a conflict unlike any other happening in the Western world at the time and, strangely, it became normal for us. Around these security measures and relentless threats, life, as troubled and downright dangerous as it was, had to go on.

We drove through big towns that were once buzzing, but which were now deserted at night, and our journeys were interrupted by the British Army checkpoints that had arrived on our streets in 1969. Those who couldn't get away from the Troubles tried to adapt a 'life goes on' attitude. People fell in love and got married; babies were born; and though Catholic and Protestants struggled to live side by side in those years, in their own communities they lived like anyone else did.

The Ramblin' Men took many risks as we toured Ireland throughout the first half of the Troubles, but people still wanted to dance and we still wanted to entertain. Somehow, despite all this, the first time I actually heard a bomb go off was in London. And I was in Manchester when it was bombed in 1996. In fact, I had been in the Arndale shopping centre only the day before.

* * *

On a lighter note, shopping was one of my favourite things to do in my spare time. In those days, I mostly shopped locally for my stage clothes, in Snooty Fox in Dungannon. But if we were away, I would shop around and enjoy the outfits that other towns had to offer. I wore glittery jackets and skirts, and I always did my own hair and make-up, unless I needed to visit a hairdresser for a cut and colour.

Changing facilities were usually very limited on the road, but in truth, I didn't mind changing in the ladies bathrooms, because I could have the odd sneaky smoke behind Tom's back and he'd have no idea. It was an ideal place for me to have a sneaky puff. Even my parents didn't know I smoked!

After the shows, we would pack up the gear and I'd talk to fans and sign autographs and pose for photos, before heading for home. Between shows, my life during the day was very ordinary. I never sat down – I was always cleaning and cooking, happy in my own wee world. Then evening would come and we'd be back on the road again.

I made many friends along the way through my music, but I never really had time for female friendships. Because of my hectic schedule, I lost touch with many of the girls I had grown up with. Looking back, I was living on love, and enjoying every moment of it.

But there was one lady, and one song, I was most fortunate to come across in 1975 – not in Nashville, but on my own home turf in Ireland. This song would be the one to take my musical career to an even higher level. That lady was Billie Jo Spears, and the song was 'Blanket on the Ground'.

Chapter Seven

Texas to Tyrone: Me and Billie Jo

The first time I heard 'Blanket on the Ground' was in August 1975, on the 'Late Night Country Show', a programme on the American Forces Network that we used to listen to on our way home from a show. The song immediately caught my attention. I thought it would be ideal for my voice and the sound we had developed in the Ramblin' Men. Tony got onto it straight away. The next morning, after a few phone calls to America, we managed to find the song and were granted permission to record it.

I was really excited about recording 'Blanket on the Ground', a song with heartfelt, interesting lyrics. Because listeners down the years had described my singing as honest and believable, I felt my voice would match this song perfectly.

I didn't know the singer of the song – Billie Jo Spears, a huge star from Beaumont in Texas, who was discovered when she was only thirteen years of age. Billie Jo had already enjoyed great success in America, and we needed to act fast before her version of 'Blanket on the Ground' properly reached our shores.

A week later, I had recorded the song, and then followed the band to Glenfarne later that evening for our gig, not having time to give a thought to the success that it might soon become.

My version of 'Blanket on the Ground' took on a life of its own. We watched it climb to No. 5 in the Irish charts, which was more than any of us had ever dreamed of. Billie Jo's recording peaked at No. 11 here in Ireland.

Later that year, we were performing at a festival in Peterborough, England, and a lady called Brenda Lee introduced me to Billie Jo Spears, who was also on the bill. Billie Jo looked amazing. She was absolutely beautiful, with her permed hairstyle and her fancy, glitzy clothes. The first words she said to me were:

'Are you the bitch who stole my song?'

'Sure isn't that my song now?' I said back to her, and we clicked instantly. She got my humour, and I got hers, and the competition was healthy and plentiful!

We had a bit of a laugh about that, and there were no hard feelings whatsoever, yet both of us knew the fierce chart battle we'd just been through, and each knew which version we were cheering on! Billie Jo told me that she'd been in a café in Derry, and when she heard the opening of the song on the radio in the background, at first she thought it was her own version. She was shocked to find out that my version was well ahead of hers in the Irish charts!

'Blanket on the Ground' was an important turning point in my career, there is no doubt about that. There was a lot of speculation, over many weeks and months, about which version was selling the most copies. Tony kept a good eye on what was happening, and made sure the success of 'Blanket on the Ground' made all the newspapers, raising my profile immensely.

We didn't have social networking of course in the 1970s. It was all down to word of mouth, newspaper interviews and that all-important radio airplay. It was all such a blessing – 'Blanket on the Ground' and the connection to Billie Jo Spears made sure plenty of that attention came my way. It's unbelievable, but even to this day, it's still the song that everyone wants to hear, no matter where in the world I go. 'Queen of the Silver Dollar' is up there too as the most requested, as is 'Ramblin' Man' and 'Truck Drivin' Woman', but it was 'Blanket on the Ground' that took my career to a completely different level and got people talking. More importantly, it got them listening!

The next time I bumped into Billie Jo Spears wasn't until the Waterfront in Belfast in 2007, and I couldn't believe the change in her appearance. Gone was the lovely curly hair and the sparkle in her eyes. She was small and extremely thin, wearing a beanie hat. She was unrecognisable, and I was told she was exhausted from travelling. The promoter, James McGarrity, had planned for us to perform 'Blanket on the Ground' together at that show, and at a few others he had lined up over the next few days, but when the time came, Billie Jo said she was simply too tired. She sat at the side of the stage in her bedroom slippers, watching me perform our song on my own. All the while I could see her, so slight and so tiny, but tapping her toes to the song that had made both of us more familiar to the public eye and ear. I was singing my heart out, determined not to let the side down of course, but wishing that Billie Jo could have found the energy to sing it with me. I understood her exhaustion, but I really couldn't get over the change in her. Perhaps she was sick, or perhaps it was just good old jet lag. I really couldn't tell.

Then, just around the middle of the song, Billie Jo found the strength to join me after all. She tip-toed out on to the centre of the stage in her slippers and began to sing! The audience went berserk with delight, and they clapped and squealed and sang along. I think the bedroom slippers added to it, and just when I thought she had run out of surprises, she stopped in the middle of the song to tell me in front of everyone that I was singing the wrong words.

'It's *slip* around, not *sleep* around!' she told me, with a cheeky nudge and a wink.

'Yes, I know it is,' I told her, 'but I like to say sleep around to spice it up!'

I was changing the words on purpose, and it gave us plenty to fool around with when singing the song from then on.

That night at the Waterfront was the beginning of our on-stage partnership, and we would go on to do six tours together over the next four years. But every time Billie Jo arrived in Ireland, she looked more and more fragile, and as she did so, we grew closer and closer as friends.

She never told me the extent of her illness, and I never probed or asked for any information. In hindsight, I think we were both too afraid to bring it up. We preferred to spend our time together laughing and joking about positive, everyday things, rather than anything darker. She became quite dependent on me when we went on the road, and I'd look after her and take her under my wing, even putting on her shoes for her when she felt too weak to do so herself.

Billie Jo visited our family home in Galbally in 2008, and I have to say, she was such fun to have around. She could be a moody wee character, though. I used to call her a 'crabbit wee bitch', and she would laugh and call me an 'old coot'.

The one thing we really disagreed on was her smoking. I had stopped smoking in 1987, and I still try to avoid being around the smell of cigarette smoke, but there was no way I could get away from it with Billie Jo. She was a serious chain-smoker, and would light up one cigarette after another if she could get away with it. We'd have to stop the tour bus constantly to let her have a puff, and sometimes the driver would threaten to put her off if she kept it up. But keep them up she did, and her insistence got us into trouble on the odd occasion!

One night in March 2009, just before we went on stage at the INEC Killarney, Billie Jo decided to have a smoke in the shower room, which was just off our dressing room. I frantically waved a towel around the room to

Fooling around with Billie Jo on the Queens of Country tour in 2011.

get rid of the smoke before the fire alarm went off, but it was too late and the fire brigade landed out to the venue. After that, she would climb on a chair and cover the smoke alarms with a plastic bag, or she'd hang out of a window to have her cigarette – you couldn't be up to her! She was a deadly wee woman for the smoking! I used to tell her she could have one cigarette only per bus journey, but as soon as she'd finished it, she'd have another one lit up, having snuck it out of the packet! As a joke, I used to put tissues up my nose, or wave a magazine around to try to get rid of the smell. She'd laugh heartily at the efforts I made to get her not to smoke so much. But no matter how delicate she became, she'd light up as and when she felt like it!

She was very witty and a lot of fun, but she definitely had her quiet moments too. There were times when she wouldn't talk to me, but would just sit there staring for some time, eventually saying:

'What's wrong with you, you old coot? Are you all right?'

She felt the cold easily, but she seemed to forget to bring a coat every time she came to Ireland, so I always ended up finding her one. Another running joke between us! She used to wear hold-up stockings, but they'd always be hanging down because she was so thin, and I'd joke and call her Nora Batty.

'These old thigh-highs, and I've no thighs!' she'd say to me, laughing.

When she was on stage and it was my time to join her, she'd call into the wings:

'Come here to me, *Philadelphia*! Help me sing this song!'

From 'Philadelphia' to 'Nora Batty', we had many names for each other, and we'd keep each other going at every turn. The audiences loved our chemistry, as did I.

Because she felt the cold so easily, she hated the windows being opened in the car when we were travelling. Even though I told her off for smoking so much, it was always in a joking way and we never, ever fell out. In fact, she confided in me about a lot of things, and we never had a cross word. She told me all about her family life in Beaumont, Texas, and her working life in Nashville. I always felt she had been disappointed by the international music industry for not recognising her achievements properly.

The last time I ever saw Billie Jo was in May 2011. We were finishing our Queens of Country tour, and she came around the back of my chair where I was sitting in our dressing room. She put her hands on my shoulders and looked at me in the mirror.

'You know something, Philly,' she said. 'I don't think I will be back here again.'

I paused and looked at her reflection in the mirror. We shared a moment right then, but I for one didn't believe her. I didn't believe that I'd never see her again, even as she stood there with tears in her eyes. She was very tired and very weak, but I just couldn't imagine her ever letting it beat her. She had lung cancer, something she never actually told me herself, but it was there, lingering always, taking my friend and making her weaker and weaker every time she came to Ireland.

'Why do you keep coming back all this way?' I asked her.

'For my family,' she told me. The only reason she continued to tour and push herself so hard was to raise money for her family before she left this world. I think now maybe she knew that was about to happen soon. But no one else did.

I have a photo taken on that last night we sang together, an image which has always stuck with me. I am at the front of the stage and I am waving goodbye to the audience, with Billie Jo doing the same just behind me. She is smiling so much and, in the print I own, she has a multi-coloured orb of light surrounding her, making her look radiant and happy. This, despite her pain of knowing what was ahead of her.

Billie Jo decided after a while that she wanted to go back to her original home place of Vidor, near Beaumont in Texas, rather than return to Nashville. I spoke to her on the phone quite often after she left me that May.

'How are you feeling now?' I asked her one day in November.

'I'm not good,' she said. 'But I'm going to fight the bugger.'

And once again I believed her. There was something about Billie Jo – you just never knew what was going on behind that tiny, sparrow-like frame and nothing would have surprised me with her. She said she could fight the bugger, and I honestly thought she would.

But fight it she couldn't, and on 14 December 2011, I got word from Texas by telephone that my good old buddy Billie Jo Spears had died of lung cancer, at the age of seventy-three. Incredulous and totally lost for words, I got the shock of my life. Though deep down we all knew it was coming, I was completely stunned. I sat in silence to let the news sink in, still hearing her cheeky laugh echo around me and seeing the radiant smile that, to me, she will always wear.

I still like to reflect on the many golden memories that Billie Jo and I collected during our friendship, and I smile as I recall them. After she died, her son sent me a little owl from her collection, which I will always cherish in her name. It sits now with pride of place in my sitting room in Galbally, and when I look at it, precious memories come flooding back: her crystal shoes, and how she carried around flat slipper-type shoes with her initials 'BJ' on them, to change into when her feet got too sore in heels; how she sang on stage in those slippers that first night in the Waterfront, and on the last night that we performed together; how she presented me with a pair the same as hers, with my initials 'PB' on them.

I still miss having Billie Jo's visits to look forward to – all our nicknames and the nights we laughed away as we moved to and from shows on our many tours across Ireland; our many late-night conversations, when she'd confide in me over a cigarette, huddled up in a big coat to protect her from the cold Irish weather.

Later, much to my delight, our friendship was sealed in a song, written by Shunie Crampsey, who called me the day after Billie Jo died. I am truly grateful that he did. Shunie said he had been at our show in the Millennium Forum in Derry, and was touched by our unique bond, both on and off the stage. He sang the words to me down the phone from Donegal, and I loved it instantly; he had captured the real essence of our friendship.

The song, 'A Tribute to Billie Jo', wasn't really intended for release. Everything happened so quickly with it; I recorded it just to send to Billie Jo's family – her sons, Tim Pierce and Kevin Jones, and her daughter, Donna Coker – in time to be played at her memorial service. Her family loved it, and it was her son Tim who put a video version on YouTube. It generated so much interest – at last count, over 100,000 views – and with the encouragement of Billie Jo's family, I just knew I had to release it as a single. In 2012, in a poll of country music DJs across Europe, it was voted the most popular airplay single in the Hotdisc Country Chart, and it was all down to Shunie's touching lyrics.

Shunie had captured us both perfectly with every word of his song, because behind all the fancy costumes, the stage lights and the fame, we really were just two country girls, from Texas and Tyrone, and when the lights went down and the crowds went away, that's exactly what we became to each other: ordinary people who lived somewhat extraordinary lives, with our hearts at home with our families.

RIP Billie Jo, my dear, dear friend. I will never forget you. I hope you are keeping warm and that you brought a coat to heaven.

Love and songs, from your friend, Philadelphia.

A Tribute to Billie Jo

A cold day in December, when the word came down the line
About a country legend, a real true friend of mine.
People they were talkin', but I sat there not a sound,
When I heard Billie Jo had finally laid the blanket down

Some songs we sang together, but yet we both made them our own.
Then we were just two country girls from Texas and Tyrone.
I prayed to God in heaven, that peace at last she'd found,
When I heard Billie Jo had finally laid the blanket down.

The friend I had in Billie Jo, again I'll never find.
She's singing that old fashioned song, and what I've got in mind,
That '57 Chevrolet, the blanket on the ground.
I cried the day my friend BJ, she laid the blanket down.

I'll be forever grateful for my time spent with you, friend.
The shows we did, the songs we sang, are sadly at an end.
But some day in the heavens we'll meet again, I know.
And we'll sing 'Blanket on the Ground', just me and Billie Jo.

The friend I had in Billie Jo, again I'll never find.

She's singing that old-fashioned song, and what I've got in mind,

That '57 Chevrolet, the blanket on the ground.

I cried the day my friend BJ, she laid the blanket down.

Shunie Crampsey, 2011

Chapter Eight

The Ray Lynam
Years

I t's always an honour to team up and sing with fellow country stars, and I am very privileged to have shared the stage with many of the finest down the years. I first met Ray Lynam in the early days of my career, when we both appeared on Margo O'Donnell's TV show in the very early 1970s.

I was rehearsing my slot in the TV studio and Ray was listening, when his manager, Sean Reilly, approached me to see if I would be interested in recording some duets with Ray. I was game of course, and agreed, but it would be twelve months before we made it to the studio, owing to our busy schedules with our own bands. Ray was a big star with the Hillbillies by then, and he was a bit like myself: always on the go! We recorded a single called 'You're the One I Can't Live Without' in 1973, and it shot up the charts, so we knew that an album of duets was going to be a good idea! In 1973, we made the album *The Two of Us*, recorded in Castleblayney. It was a roaring success, but we never did get to tour it, because of our heavy workloads. Our paths crossed many times after that, and we ventured into the studio again in 1974 to record a second album, *Together ... Again!* We sang together at the International Country Music Festival in Wembley the same year, but we still couldn't manage to find the time to tour the duets we had recorded, which I always thought was a pity given their massive success.

Recording with Ray was an opportunity to showcase my voice to an audience who enjoyed what we both did. I always enjoyed the challenge of working with new people whenever the opportunity came around. Of course, I'm delighted to be in such demand, both with the band and as a singer in my own right.

Finally, in 1975, after doing the rounds with Hank Locklin and his band, we ventured off on our own tour, starting at the very top of Scotland and ending right at the bottom of England. The singles we released, 'Jeannie's Afraid of the Dark' and 'My Elusive Dreams', won us the title of Europe's Top Country Duo at the Wembley Festival that year.

'I think our success was due to a novelty effect we had back then,' says Ray. 'We were doing something that no one else really was in these parts at the time, and it was like that from the start – we just had chemistry and it was always fun.

'We regularly took a fit of the giggles on stage. In fact, one night in Portsmouth, I recall that the band played the entire song and we never managed to sing one word of it because we were laughing so hard. That's the type of thing we'd find happening, and maybe that's why people liked us singing together so much. It was, and still is, great craic.

'I was totally sold on [Philomena's] voice the moment I heard it. I've always loved her voice – she has a big voice, and an even bigger heart. She's a mighty character, very funny, and she commands the whole stage the moment she sets foot on it. I think the secret to our success together was our mutual respect for one another. Individually, as well as that magnificent voice, I think Philomena is still the Queen of Country because she is of the people. People relate to her and I tend to stand back and let her get on with it! She is easy to work with, and people identify with her. All in all, she's a remarkable woman for her age – just don't tell her I said that!'

Ray Lynam and I collecting awards for Europe's Top Country Duo at Wembley in 1975.

I'll let on I never heard the age bit, Ray, but I'll take the rest, thanks! We sure did have some good old times, and thankfully still do.

As the years passed by, Ray and I managed to squeeze in a few other albums, which country fans continued to enjoy. These were the compilations *We Go Together Again* (Sonus, 1984) and *Country Stars* (Homespun, 1984), and an album of new material in 1985 on Ritz Records called *Simply Divine*. We became known as a reliable combination, and country music fans in the UK and Ireland seemed to love our sound, with all of our albums being received really well.

We did have the odd argument, but only in a professional way, and we never fell out on a personal level. Maybe we disagreed on what songs to put on the albums and which ones to rule out. There was a level of respect there between Ray and me that has allowed for many revivals, including the Country Royalty tour in March 2017, where we successfully toured theatres in Ireland backed by my son's band, the Aidan Quinn Band.

By far the greatest compliment that Ray and I could ever have received was to appear in The Pogues's song 'A Pair of Brown Eyes', written by Shane MacGowan in 1985. I don't remember where I was when I first heard their song on the radio, but I do remember wondering if I was hearing things. After looking into it, I realised that Shane MacGowan was indeed singing about me and my old partner, and I admit it did make me smile. I have yet to see 'A Pair of Brown Eyes' performed live, or to meet Shane MacGowan himself. I'd just love to hear the story behind the song, but sure there's still time for that. Maybe one day soon.

Chapter Nine

1978: A Year of Great Loss

My eldest brother Patsy and I were always very close.

He was what we called 'a real character', and he kept all on earth going with his wit and charm. Everyone, including me, loved him very much. Patsy followed my career on a daily basis, and he'd phone me every single day to ask how my gig went the night before. He even drove to Carrickmore once to check how many empty chip wrappers there were lying about the streets, so he could gauge whether or not we'd had a good crowd in when we played the hall there.

My sisters and my mother often joked that if there was an awkward way of doing something, Patsy would find it, but he'd always get it done. He had many, many jobs in his day. One of his first was running the barber's from our shop at home in Pomeroy. He would cut hair all night; there was no such thing as a quitting time. He had one of those cutthroat razors, and was very skilled at the job. Sometimes when things were quiet, we'd have to go looking for him in the ball alley when he'd disappear to play handball. The barber shop became an extension of our own home, and earned the reputation of a 'céilí house', where many men would land after spilling out of the pubs as late as 10pm. Patsy would be mad to get out to the dances himself, but those men would sit with him for ages and tell him all their problems. He was known as a caring and gentle soul, and he always had an ear for everyone.

When Margaret and Angela were doing their driving tests, no one knew they had it booked. Somehow Patsy found out, but didn't tell them he knew. Instead, he quietly offered them each his own car to take for a test run the night before, just so they'd have the confidence to do their test. Such was the type of him, always looking out for his younger siblings and wanting the best for them.

He drove a Bedford van for a while. One day Plunkett and Daddy were driving it up to the farm at the Curragh, and on the way they got a flat tyre. Daddy reached into the back for the spare, but it too was in shreds. You can imagine the reaction of my father, who was always so well prepared and would not have heard of such carelessness. What there was in the back of the van, though, was a grand, fully made-up bed. Patsy was all equipped for travelling around in many ways, just not in the usual ways of other folk!

As a footballer for Pomeroy Plunketts GFC, they say Patsy was light-ning-quick, and he was never once cautioned on the field, which says a lot about his character. He was known as 'Shorty', but what he lacked in height he made up for in speed. He was also a county medallist for playing handball, even going on to earn himself an Ulster title and making us all very proud.

'Handball is where we live, life is just a place where we spend time between games,' said the Canadian ice hockey player Fred Shero. He is quoted in a book recently published for the Pomeroy Plunketts GFC's centenary year. In it my nephew Martin, Patsy's son, recalls:

'I was born on 12 June 1965. My father was scheduled to play in the Ulster Junior Doubles final and he left my mother in the labour ward to play. In fact, as my mother pointed out, he left to cut hair and then go on to play in the final. He won that game, by the way.'

Patsy was a dedicated football and handball player, no one could question that, but he was also very devoted to his family. When he met his wife, Alice, he couldn't have been any kinder to her, and they went on to have five beautiful children – Martin, Anne, Conor, Fiona and Louise – for whom he worked very hard. Any time he came into our shop, he would always ask for a treat for Alice, who is a lovely, modest, quiet and unassuming lady.

Patsy had tried all sorts of jobs throughout the 1960s, including driving a school bus for a while. He'd wash the bus in The Diamond in the middle of Pomeroy village for all to see, much to the delight of the local children, who would watch him or sometimes give a helping hand.

His barber shop, opened in 1966, became a big part of the community, almost like an extension to the local pub, where many a game of poker was played. Problems were discussed there too, as Patsy was a renowned listener and advisor to everyone. He was an excellent barber, trained by Sean Skelton in Dungannon. He was very popular, and I never knew him to have a closing time, as customers called to him day and night. If he wasn't there when a customer came by, Mary could step in. But one day, she was away too. Plunkett decided to give it a go, but he hadn't a clue what he was doing.

Patsy was also a chimney sweep at one stage! Patsy took much pride in having a mobile home in Bundoran in County Donegal. All the locals loved to call with him, and he'd give them bread and jam. One day, an old rope that Daddy used around the farm, called 'the tether', went missing and it turned out that it was up in Bundoran, being used to tie up Patsy's mobile home!

The Pomeroy Accordion Band, late 1960s. My father stands in the back row, second from the left, and my brother Patsy is kneeling in the front row, third from the right.

That was his way – you'd never know what he would be up to. My sister Margaret was the one he could wind up the most. As teenagers, Angela and my cousin Pat didn't like anyone to know they worked in the local factory, so when Patsy would see them coming, he'd announce as loud as he could:

'Here come the factory girls!'

The two girls could do nothing more than laugh, and he'd sometimes make them laugh until their sides were sore. When we were younger, Plunkett and Patsy would have kept all the craic going at the dinner table, and there was never a dull moment when he was around.

I believe his interest in business came from my father, who was also a fine entrepreneur. Patsy followed in his footsteps by booking some of the biggest bands in the country, such as the Indians, Brian Coll and the Buckaroos and many more, to play Pomeroy Hall throughout the 1970s. He took immense pride in announcing in 1978 that there was going to be a massive festival in Pomeroy that June, and that he would be the chief organiser.

'This town will never see a weekend like this again,' he told us all, as he arranged everything from football tournaments to showband concerts and dances. It really was going to be the most impressive carnival Pomeroy had ever witnessed, and there was a lot of excitement in every corner of our home and on every corner of the street.

Patsy's festival was a distraction we all needed that summer, because only six months before, on 21 December 1977, our family had been dealt a devastating blow. My sister Angela had lost her two-year-old child, a wee girl called Mary, to meningitis. We were just beginning to pick ourselves up from the shock of that when Patsy took sick one day, two weeks before his big event. He didn't make a fuss, and drove himself to hospital, and none of us believed it to be anything serious. He couldn't have known that he would never return to his beloved Pomeroy again, and that the big weekend he had planned, 'the biggest weekend that Pomeroy would ever see', would actually be the occasion of his own funeral.

My precious brother and friend, Patsy, died from a clot on his lung around 5am on 26 June 1978. He was just forty-one, and left behind his devastated wife Alice, and their five young children. I had been travelling home from a gig in Gort, County Galway, around that time, and I remember seeing a massive flash of light cross the sky. I'd never seen anything like it before, but I found out in recent years that my brother Plunkett, who was on his way to the hospital in Belfast at the same time, saw the very same flash of light when coming through Dungannon. My sister Angela witnessed something very similar on the night her darling daughter Mary died six months before. To this day I don't know what it was, but I remember feeling that something strange was going on. When I got home to Galbally, my biggest fears had come true, and my father rang to tell me the most horrific news.

I couldn't believe he was gone. I recall just standing there, dropping the phone and wailing and screaming in total dismay. He was too young to die, and it was all too sudden to take in. I screeched and cried for the big brother I had loved so much, and for his poor wife and children to whom he had been so devoted. I cried for all his dreams and plans that were snatched from him in the prime of his life. How could life be so cruel?

Needless to say, the loss of Patsy nearly killed Mammy and Daddy.

I will never forget the sight of my father carrying his eldest son's coffin through the village, as the Pomeroy Accordion Band of which he and Patsy were members played the famous tune 'The Mountains of Pomeroy'. Crowds lined the streets and bowed their heads for the loss of a young husband, a father, a son, a sportsperson and a local businessman who had dedicated so much of his life to his community.

It was indeed the biggest weekend Pomeroy had seen in a long time, that's for sure, just as he had predicted, but it was also truly the saddest. The funeral cortège stretched over a mile from the Church of the Assumption right through the town. It united the people of Pomeroy with those from much further afield, as crowds from the GAA, the music world and all our friends and family gathered to say goodbye.

A tribute published in a local paper at the time said that Patsy's death had left 'an unfathomable void in every aspect of life in the village of Pomeroy. Shorty was not, as the (nick)name suggests, physically big, but the greatness of the man lay in the humanitarian qualities he so abundantly possessed. Patsy had a commitment to life based on the great Christian commandment of love, and his quiet and unassuming nature hid a strength of character that left an indelible mark on all who knew him.'

Patsy was godfather to my own firstborn, Mary. He used to sing the song 'Brown Girl in the Ring' when he'd see her and she'd cry when he wasn't there, asking me to play it. I played it for her one day after he passed, and tried to dance around the kitchen with her in my arms just like he used to, but the pain was too much and I sobbed my heart out as the music blared in the background.

In fact, I still can't listen to that song without it bringing a tear to my eye and a deep soreness to my heart.

My big brother, one of my biggest supporters and best friends, will never be forgotten.

Chapter Ten

Motherhood

I had always loved babies, and would consider myself a very maternal person, with fond memories of looking after my youngest brother with care and pride. So as soon as Tom and I were married in 1974, we couldn't wait to start a family.

The first half of the 1970s were a busy time for us professionally, as the Ramblin' Men soared to success, but I had been on the road for almost fourteen years by then, so it felt like the right time for me to have a baby. Also, I was in my mid-thirties, and I could hear my biological clock ticking.

To my delight, things happened fairly quickly, and it was with immense joy that I told Tom I was pregnant. Of course, he was thrilled to bits. We were very excited and I couldn't wait to tell my friends and family while I waited for the first twelve weeks to pass.

But it wasn't to be.

Exactly twelve weeks into my pregnancy, at home in my kitchen in Galbally, I got terrible pains in my stomach and had to be rushed to hospital, where I miscarried. Tom and I were devastated; all our plans for our new arrival went out the window, and we were faced with a loss that we were not prepared for at all.

For a long time afterwards, I was very down and depressed, with an overwhelming sense of loss that I'd had no chance to anticipate. But I didn't and I couldn't talk too much about it – back then, miscarriage was a very taboo subject. Women were expected to get up and get on with it, so that's exactly what I did. But I couldn't quieten the anger I felt inside at losing my first precious baby.

I struggled to understand why it had happened – did I do something wrong, or something that was against the rules of expecting a baby? Was it because I was so busy all the time? Should I have slowed down and taken it easier, to give the baby a chance? I felt so guilty and had so many questions and no information about why this had happened to me. I went to the doctor, looking for some answers, but his attitude did nothing to help my inner sadness. He told me I wasn't the first to lose a baby, and I wouldn't be the last!

Miscarriage is often considered 'one of those things', but when it happened to me, I was totally unprepared for the sadness that it brought my way. Thankfully, the Ramblin' Men were riding high on the success of 'Blanket On the Ground', which took my mind off it a little and I was able to go back to work fairly soon, but it never really left me. I still think about it to this day.

Then, thankfully, in early 1976, I found out that I was pregnant a second time. Once again, in the early weeks, the pains came, but for this one I was adamant that I would stop all appearances and rest until I was out of the twelve-week danger zone. So for two whole weeks, I played no music and for the first time in many, many years, I had to just stop. It was very strange, but my pregnancy and my own health had to come first. I knew it was for the best and there was no way I was going to risk the same thing happening to me again. Tom and the band played on, and continued to gig through-out Ireland without me. I remember him coming home one night from a show in Ballymena with a curry for me from a place I loved. He thought he was doing such a good turn, but the very smell of it turned my guts, and it ended up in the bin!

After a fortnight of complete bed rest, I was given the all-clear from the doctor and I was able to go back to work, but the sickness stayed for quite a while. The only thing that distracted me from the nausea was singing. How about that for the power of music? It can even distract from morning sickness!

I totally loved being pregnant. The fashion for pregnant women in 1970s Ireland was very different to what it is now. There were no such things as clingy tops – as soon as a woman found out she was expecting she would put on smock tops or dresses. I got a lovely blue dress especially made. I loved it so much that I got another one made in lime green, and then another one in pink. They all came in handy for being on stage, as there was no way I was ever going to show my bump – it just wasn't the done thing in those days.

I stayed on stage until October 1976, and in December I went into hos-pital, where they induced my labour. However, after waiting all day, there was nothing happening. They were different times then, when men really weren't expected to hang about for the delivery, so Tom left for work at

5pm, and at 1am, I was petrified when they took me for an emergency cae-sarean section. It was like something from a television show, and it scared the life out of me, as they wheeled me at speed down the corridor, prepping me for surgery along the way. I remember a priest arriving at the bottom of the bed, and I had to sign a consent form, but I could barely see it I was in so much pain.

Our beautiful, healthy daughter Mary was born, weighing a whopping 9 lbs 10 oz, and she had a big mop of black hair and an adorable, chubby face. I was thrilled to bits. I had big plans for Mary: she would be my best friend and we would go everywhere together. I was honestly on top of the world. Tom arrived shortly after the gig, and he too was over the moon with his new baby girl.

'She looks like me,' he said, glowing as he stared down at her ,and I had to agree. She was very much her daddy's girl.

I was brought back to the ward and the next morning, some photogra-phers from the local papers arrived to take our picture. I remember Davy Dougal turning up from the *Tyrone Courier* and I was barely fit to look at him, never mind to smile! The photo appeared in the newspaper that week, and the story of Mary's birth even made UTV News. I stayed in hospital until Boxing Day, and I have to say I had the best craic when I was in there. I bet there aren't too many women who would say that about their stay in a maternity unit! The amount of cards and messages I got was overwhelming, and the sister on the ward put them all around the bed and taped them to the wall above me. They had come from all corners of Ireland and further afield, and it really helped my recovery as I read through them all.

I couldn't laugh after the operation, but was fit to make decorations for Christmas once I got over the first few days, and soon I was back giggling and laughing with the staff and we had a mighty Christmas dinner. Whoever complains about hospital food never had their dinner in South Tyrone Hospital on Christmas Day, because I have to say it was top of the range! Or maybe I was just very ready for it! I felt like I was on holidays for the ten days I spent there, because of the lovely people and staff that I met, especially a nurse called Mary Kelly. Come to think of it, it was also probably because I had been travelling every night for so many years that it was nice to stop and sample another side of life. A slower pace for a while.

We brought Mary home to Galbally on Boxing Day, and Tom was out again that night, playing with the Ramblin' Men across the country. I suppose I just took motherhood in my stride, and I think I adapted very naturally to my new role. I also needed to work, and I was back on stage by February, but I always made sure we got home straight after the gigs. I had a fantastic childminder in Dympna Donaghy, who looked after Mary at night and let me get to work, and then I would spend all day with her. A bit like working night shifts, I suppose, and I was already well used to the late nights and early starts.

It was around this time, early 1977, when our good friend Rose Murphy came to stay with us. Rose was one of eleven siblings and their family home nearby was being renovated, so they all needed somewhere to stay for a while until the work was done. Rose would go on to become an important part of our family: she grew very close to Mary, and we didn't want to let her go!

I remember one Christmas Mary got a Barbie house which came with a swimming pool, but Santa forgot the batteries. She cried non-stop for the whole day. Being my first child, I imagined that we would do all sorts together, but as soon as she hit primary school she had no time for her poor old mother after all! She was what we call a 'run the roads', and loved going to friends' houses on her céilí or to any event going on – and still does!

With Aidan, who came along in November 1979, I remember being very big – when I'd go in to the hospital for my check-up I was so huge I had to reverse into the cubicle! I mind one night on stage in Castleblayney singing the national anthem, and he gave me a massive kick that made me clasp my bump, much to the amusement of the women in the audience. I worked as long as I was fit to during that pregnancy and, despite my size, I sang on and it didn't do me any harm. Aidan was born in a planned caesarean section, which was a lot less dramatic than Mary's arrival. I was prepared for theatre and knocked out, and the next thing I felt was some-one tapping at my face.

'Philly, wake up! Wake up! You've a lovely big healthy baby boy!'

It was Mary O'Hara, Dano's wife (who worked in South Tyrone Hospital), waking me up with the great news. Sure enough, Aidan was indeed a big lad – so long, in fact, that everyone on the ward came to see him. The press arrived again to take our photo and Aidan even made the TV sports news, with the reporter announcing, 'Begley's boy weighs in at 11 lbs 1 oz!'

Once again, our son was the spitting image of Tom, with a big head of black hair. His name was suggested by one of the nurses in the hospital. Afterwards, Dympna continued to help us out at home, which allowed me to fulfil my work commitments at night, and I was back on stage by March of 1980.

My youngest child, Carol, was born in 1981, in South Tyrone Hospital, just like her siblings. She was the smallest of the three, at 8 lb 10 oz – still a healthy baby nonetheless! She arrived on 18 May, and she was named after Pope Karl, whose birthday was the same day. I wasn't very well after Carol's birth, and had to be given several pints of blood. I was thirty-seven years old, and I was considered an 'older mother', so I had no ambitions to have any more. Tom and I were happy that our family was complete.

As the children grew up, I can't say I was too strict a parent, but I wasn't too easy-going either. I could make a lot of noise with the threat of a wooden spoon or a wee tap on the backside when they were a bit bigger, but they never gave me much bother, and I've had a lovely relationship with all three of them over the years.

There were moments when we had to instil some discipline in our house, and I tried to be strict with my children when it was necessary, especially

Carol, Mary and Aidan at school in St Joseph's Primary School, Galbally.

during their teens. I remember Mary sobbing her heart out at the top of the stairs when she wasn't allowed to go to discos.

When she was a teenager, Mary thought she was in big trouble once. It all started with a gathering of friends at our house when Tom and I were both away.

'I was at secondary school at the time and I decided to have a bit of a party back at our house,' says Mary. 'Mammy had been presented with a specially commissioned Tyrone Crystal crown a while before to celebrate thirty years in show business, and it was sitting pride of place among hundreds of other ornaments, trophies and prizes that she had gathered down the years. I knew this one was always special as it had been presented to her by Daniel O'Donnell. There were three balls on top of the crown and it sat on a velvet cushion. My friends and I were playing music so loud that the crystal crown vibrated and one of the balls of the crown fell off! There was panic all around and one of the boys was tasked to take the crown to Tyrone Crystal the next day to have it fixed. It cost £50, which was a fortune to us teenagers, but we gathered it up and the crown was fixed as good as new.

'The next day, my friend Damian, who had gone to collect the repaired crown, was bringing it back to our house so that we could get it back in its place before Mammy and Daddy arrived home. All was going according to plan and we were delighted with ourselves, but just as Damian put his finger on our doorbell, the bottom of its box fell through and the crown smashed into smithereens on the doorstep!

'You can imagine the despair as we swept up all the tiny shatterings of crystal with a dustpan and brush and I put it in a plastic carrier bag and hid it in my room, terrified of how I was going to break the news to Mammy on her return. It stayed there for days and still she didn't notice it gone. Then a few weeks passed and I was going through internal hell wondering when I was going to be caught out, so I decided to come clean.

'Mammy was standing at the sink peeling spuds when I approached her and placed the plastic bag on the side of the worktop, and she asked what it was. When I told her, she said absolutely nothing, which was worse than her shouting or punishing me in some way. Instead, as I walked out of the kitchen, I could hear her sobbing, and that broke my heart even more. I was so sorry that I had actually made my mammy cry, yet she never said a word to me about it since.'

It's funny when you hear their versions of such stories after all these years, but I do remember that feeling when Mary confessed to the fate of the Tyrone Crystal crown. On a night in 1992, when I thought I was doing a charity appearance in Dublin, I was surprised to find all my friends and family gathered to mark my thirtieth anniversary as a singer. When it was presented to me, Daniel was holding the crown very carefully, and as he passed it across to me, he whispered in my ear:

'I broke a ball, so be careful,' and we both burst out laughing.

So poor Mary and her friends didn't really break the ball at all – it was already loose. If they'd just left it as it was, they'd have saved themselves weeks of worry, not to mention the crown itself being totally smashed up in the end! The crown has since been replaced thanks to Gary Currie, a local accordian player who worked for Tyrone Crystal. All's well that ends well.

* * *

Aidan enjoyed tipping around the farm with his daddy, and anything to do with music. Soon we discovered that music really was his first love, and he had no interest in school whatsoever. We bought him a drum kit from Danny Hughes's Music Shop in Blackrock, County Louth, when he was very young. We were at a wedding in the ballroom opposite the shop and popped in to have a look, and we ended up bringing the drum kit home. Aidan kept it in his bedroom, and when Tom would settle down at night to watch the 6 o'clock news, the battering would start from upstairs and we'd get no peace for the rest of the evening. But Aidan was in his element.

'I used to sit beside Patsy Tweedy, who was the drummer in Mammy's band Shotgun in the 1980s, and I would watch him in awe,' recalls Aidan. 'I knew then, that's what I wanted to do, and I was only about nine or ten at the time. I was fascinated by the whole business and when I was asked to fill out forms in secondary school on career ideas, I would always say I wanted to work in music. I suppose I learned from the best after all!'

Carol was very modest and timid, and kept on my tail at all times – very different to her big brother and sister! I remember her learning to ride her bike. Off she set down the hill, but forgot to pull the brakes and ended up doing a tumble into a wall.

Carol was a very cuddly child, and she was easily carried around, which is maybe the reason why she never left my side for years! I always remember looking down and seeing Carol beside me no matter what I was doing at home. She was such a modest wee girl, and I enjoyed every minute of her.

'I never got into any trouble,' Carol laughs now. 'That's why I can claim I'm the favourite!'

* * *

Every year for nineteen years, I took the children to Pontins in Southport, England, around the time of the Irish Music Festival, when Irish ex-pats would come out in their droves to hear country music from home. We made such brilliant memories there. For the children, there were swimming pools, wall climbing, outdoor games, boating pools and pitch & putt. The children would spend their days out and about around the camp. Some years, we took friends with us, but they also made a lot of friends there. When they got older, Aidan admitted that he had had his first grown-up drink in Pontins at the age of seventeen! There was a corner at the resort called Philomena's Corner (named after me!), which was a meeting point. We were standing there one night and Aidan offered to buy me a drink, and then he ordered a second one for himself, much to my surprise.

'Ma, it's like this,' he said. 'Do you want me to drink this here, or do you want me to drink it outside?'

I hadn't a clue how to respond! It was the way he said it!

Mary was bridesmaid for one of the girls, Ann Marie, who she met at Pontins, and Ann Marie used to stay with us in Galbally too. Many a night's fun we had with them, and they still keep in touch to this day.

Despite our hectic schedules, Tom and I were at home a lot, apart from one or two overseas tours a year, which we made sure to schedule away from family occasions. Unless there was a UK or US tour, I was home every day when the children came in from school, and they never returned to an empty house. Dympna and Claire Donnelly were a real help when we were performing, staying overnight with the children, but I really didn't rely on anyone else to look after them during the day. I was a working mother, except my job wasn't nine to five. While I managed everything at home, Tom maintained the farm. We worked hard together to balance the outside world of showbiz with the home life our children deserved, away from the limelight.

There were things I certainly did miss out on, but that was part of my business and thankfully my children don't seem too annoyed about it at all. I wasn't there on Mary's first day at school, for example. She was taken there by Dympna's sister, but she says it was no big deal and she knew no different. She also remembers fondly a purple tracksuit I brought her all the way from America.

'I went to primary school with this grand purple tracksuit on, and no one in my class had ever seen the like of it. When they heard it was from America and that my mammy had bought it there, it seemed even more special, and they all wanted to touch it. We had no school uniform at the time, and I remember my friend Colette Donnelly insisting she got to try it on. In fact I am almost sure that I came home in her clothes that day, because she didn't want to take it off!'

However, one of my biggest regrets was missing Aidan's confirmation in 1990, because I couldn't get a flight home from Scotland, where I was on tour with Ray Lynam. It totally broke my heart. Looking back, I really should have cancelled, but by the time I had realised that the dates clashed, the tour had sold out and it was too late.

They each remember how their father did a lot for them, to let me concentrate on my career.

'We are so lucky to have had two loving parents who were willing to make adjustments to their own lives to give us the best life possible, and I think we're better people now for it,' says Carol.

Aidan agrees that Tom and I are a good team. 'Ma looks after me very well, I have to say, and always has. She was always a fantastic cook, and she is still obsessed with what we had to eat in a day and also what her grandchildren eat. Daddy wears the trousers, and when we wouldn't get up for school, Mammy could call us many times, but all it took was for him to shout once and we'd all be out of bed like rockets.' He also remembers the 1916 celebrations concert I did in the Bord Gáis Energy Theatre in Dublin in 2016. I arrived just in time to sing 'Come by the Hill' (while most of the other artists had been there rehearsing all day), and the next morning I was back in Galbally making Tom his breakfast at 8am.

Our friend Rose has been with us since around the time Mary was born, and she remains a constant in all of our lives. Rose is like a sister to me, and like an aunt to my children, who adore her.

'Rose is the one who *does* spoil us,' says Mary. 'She spoils our own children now too, and to be honest she keeps all of us sane!'

'She is like a sister to us all,' says Aidan. 'She was always a support to Mammy and she is country music-mad. Our parents always wanted us to have a familiar face to come home to and while Rose was never officially our nanny, she was a great support to us all and we loved it.'

* * *

My children used to love watching me get ready for work, and one of Mary's earliest memories of her mother is sitting on the bed and looking on as I put rollers in my hair.

'I was very small at the time and I would watch her put on her make up; then in later years my friends and I would dress up in her clothes, which was great fun. It's not everyone who could say there was a blue Elvis-style suit in their mother's closet, all the way from Nashville!'

Carol (and Aidan!) liked to dress up in my stage clothes too. She would go through a cupboard up the stairs that contained all my old clothes, put them on. Then she and her big brother would play 'bands', which meant pretending they were going to gigs and changing into my dresses to go on stage.

My children never thought of their childhoods as any different to anyone else's. When they were very young, they never knew much about my being away, as I'd always leave when they were in bed and be back by the time they woke up the next morning. Sometimes I would take them to events, and I remember Aidan singing 'Dear Santa' with me on stage once. This was the saddest song ever, but he loved it because it mentioned Santa!

Carol, Mary and Aidan help dad Tom with a song in the family kitchen.

Although I didn't see it at the time, my children may have been treated differently because of my job, but that does seem natural and thankfully nothing too offensive was ever said or done to them. Mary admits to being a bit embarrassed to say at school that her mammy was a country singer … Country music wasn't so cool in the 1980s.

'I think it has a much better reputation now, and people seem to get excited when I say that Philomena Begley is my mum', says Mary. 'But back then it definitely wasn't something I wanted to tell everyone. One day we'd be picked up from school in a Philomena Begley-branded tour bus, and the next day it could be a tractor. But sure it was all good fun!'

There was one incident that really was embarrassing, though. That was when the *Sunday World* newspaper printed a picture of a lady who looked a lot like me, scantily clad and in a very seductive pose. The headline said something like, 'Philly as you've never seen her before.' I did think it was funny, but not for my children, who had to go to school the next day. It would surely come up among their peers.

'I was mortified,' Mary recalls. 'But I do remember Daddy joking that he knew instantly it wasn't her, because the woman in the paper had far bigger boobs, and we all got a laugh out of that. I can't even remember if anyone in school passed any remarks, but to me it was the end of the world.'

While Mary was often able to laugh these things off, for Aidan it was different. He was teased a lot in school, and one lad used to sing every time he saw him, and it was done in a scoffing way, in a bid to embarrass him. As it happens, the same people who scoffed back then actually grew up listening to my music, and they now sing a very different tune!

'They all saw Philomena Begley as a star,' says Aidan. 'But to me she was just Mammy. Some were jealous, I think.'

One teacher picked on him constantly, and I think it was a kind of power trip for him because he believed Aidan thought of himself as special. But that was never the case. My children may have been financially secure because of my job, but they were never spoiled.

When they went to secondary school especially, everyone thought they must live in a big mansion, with servants and maids, but then they'd come to our house and see me making the dinner in my apron. Even when it came to dinner money or pocket money, they never got anything extra just for the sake of it. Tom and I tried to instil a respect for money into our children. We didn't want to be extravagant with them, but at the same time we wouldn't let them go without. It was definitely a more ordinary upbringing, than any sort of silver spoon-type existence.

Aidan and Mary shared their first car, a ten-year-old Clio, and it lasted them for years. It was up to them to figure out whose turn it was to have it. Of course, they had the odd row over it, but there was no way they were getting a car each – they had to just work around it. They had weekend jobs around their school work, just like everyone else their age, so they definitely weren't indulged in a materialistic way, not a chance.

My children seem to know me better than anyone else. They have had some extraordinary moments with me and because of my work: the time the 'Neighbours' actor Stefan Dennis, during a visit to Ireland, publicly announced his wish to meet me; the time 'Lifelines' featured me in a kind of Irish version of 'This Is Your Life'; and the concerts to celebrate my thirty, forty and fifty years in show business. Carol says that when I sing 'How Great Thou Art' and an audience goes mad with applause, it always makes her want to stand up and shout 'That's my mammy!'

I was delighted and honoured to spend some time with Pam Lewis back in 1993, when she was managing Garth Brooks at the peak of his career. Garth was performing at the Point Theatre in Dublin (renamed the 3Arena), and Pam kindly sent me some VIP tickets to go to the show, so I took Mary, Aidan and Carol along. We were shown to our seats, which were right beside Albert Reynolds, who was Taoiseach at the time. As we made our way to them, we could hear some of the audience whisper my name, and the children couldn't believe it.

'The next thing was,' remembers Carol, 'the whispers rippled throughout the audience of a few thousand people and before we knew it the entire crowd were on their feet, giving her a standing ovation. Again, I wanted to shout, "That's my mammy," as I was bursting with pride.'

Aidan and I are similar in that we both like being recognised, and for me it's certainly just a way of life, now that strangers who are fans will approach me to say hello. Fame really doesn't faze me to the degree it might faze others. Mary was always disappointed when I got home from concerts or chat shows with Dolly Parton, Tammy Wynette, Sir Tom Jones, Boyzone or whoever without their autographs. I would just laugh and say, 'Sure they didn't ask me for mine!'

It's an ongoing joke in our house that Aidan is my blue-eyed boy, and my children carry on about which one is the favourite, but of course they are all unique in their own ways: Mary, our firstborn; Aidan, the only boy; and Carol, the baby. They each have their own special title! I'm delighted that my children have positive memories of growing up in Galbally. We are very close, and it's been such fun reminiscing with them while writing this book.

Finding a work–life balance as a professional singer and a mum of three certainly wasn't always easy, but I am very lucky to have been able to make it work, and that they are happy, healthy and grateful children, with whom

I can reminisce and reflect. Having a solid family life is something I will never take for granted. I know it allowed me to follow my dreams at all stages of my career – that took me all over the world, from the green fields of Ireland to the bright lights of the United States of America.

Chapter Eleven

American Dreams and Football Teams!

Philomena Begley is now Ireland's and indeed Europe's top Female Recording Artiste. Her early showbiz years were more concerned with live performances but having achieved her first number one chart hit in 1974, more effort and time was devoted to the recording aspect of her career. A new record label, Spin Records, was established on the strength of Phil's selling power and a recipe for slick country recordings was quickly established.

A succession of number one singles was surpassed only by sales of her albums and Philomena is now the proud owner of several silver, gold and

platinum discs. Her recording popularity is purely based on country music
with particular emphasis given to gospel and truckin'. She is forever willing
to experiment with new material and to have Philomena Begley record a
newly penned number is a sign that a songwriter has 'arrived'. Philomena
has recorded in Ireland, London and Nashville and having already
conquered Europe, it is now only a matter of time before she makes the same
impact in America, the Mecca of all country music markets.

Entertainment News, August 1978

By the time the Ramblin' Men marked their fourth anniversary on the
road, we had multiple awards under our belts and the media couldn't get
enough of us. My first major award came in 1973, when I was voted top
female singer nationally. I went on to present my own shows on BBC,
UTV and RTÉ. One of the crowning achievements of my early career
came in 1974, when I was the only Irish female singer to represent my
country at the International Country Music Festival in Wembley – the
event where I would first meet Billie Jo Spears. After this, I made three

At home with some of my awards in the 1970s.

subsequent appearances on this show, and in 1976, I received the top European Country Artiste award, which was presented to me on stage in front of 12,000 people.

In 1975, the boxer-turned-singer Joe Frazier came to Dundrum Town in County Down, to perform a concert and dance show organised by the late Jack Kielty (father of comedian and TV host Patrick). I had the honour of being a special guest on the bill. 'Big Jack' was a real gentleman and quite a character, and it was lovely to meet Joe Frazier, who was big news at the time.

I enjoyed doing TV work as it offered me many new challenges. It's a lot of work for a singer to communicate as well as sing, and the live setting of some of the shows left no room for mistakes. But it did my confidence the world of good. Working with the band, and with people I knew and trusted like Ray Lynam, was a safe, secure environment for me, and it was good to step out of my comfort zone every now and then and keep raising the bar for my personal best.

Top Rank Entertainments, under the watchful eye of my manager, Tony Loughman, was going from strength to strength, and even though I was the first artist to be signed to the company, there were many other well-known names and faces carving out a career in country music on the Irish scene by this point. Top Spin Records, an offshoot of Tony's talent management company, had been established on the strength of the selling power of Philomena Begley and Her Ramblin' Men, and a standard for slick country recordings was quickly established.

There was camaraderie and there was, of course, healthy competition. One of the more enjoyable downtime competitions, away from the microphones and bright lights of the stages and dance halls, was a weekly

Monday night football match, organised by Tony's team at different venues across Ireland in aid of various charities.

The players were known as the Top Rank Superstars, and we had both a ladies' and a men's team, who kitted out to give the games their best shot. The men's team featured county stars such Mick O'Dwyer, James McCartan, Dan McCartan, Paddy Doherty and Brian McEniff, while singer Mary Lou

The Top Rank Superstars all set to play football in the USA, 1978.

was on our team, as were Susan McCann and Anne and Jan Lynch of Anne, Shelly and the Marines. Bernie Gilroy, Tony's PA, was in goal, but she ended up with a black eye on one occasion and that soon put her off!

Another outlet for the Top Rank family was its weekly magazine,

Entertainment News, which informed country music fans of gigs and snippets and news of their favourite stars. We didn't have Google back in those good old days, so to find something out, you had to wait until it was printed in a magazine or a newspaper. *Entertainment News* was popular and well received, with many letters to the editor coming in with enquiries about where such-and-such was playing next. It seems strange now, when you think how easily and quickly we can find information nowadays.

One of my roles was to write a column called 'Country Corner', a wee update on the music scene from my point of view, with a bit of news from my home life thrown in for good measure. My writing, football and music could all go hand-in-hand – maybe I should have stuck to my real job, but all in all, it was a clever way to round up my week, and keep up with what was going on with the other bands too!

There were many bands to-ing and fro-ing on Irish roads, always trying to keep up with busy schedules so it was no surprise that the odd accident took place. News of anyone getting hurt was always the last thing we wanted to hear. I remember in the same week, both Brendan Bowyer (the 'Big Daddy' of the Irish showband scene) and Susan McCann's band were each involved in car accidents. While Brendan and company got away lightly, poor Susan was thrown through the windscreen and was taken to hospital where she received stitches to her head.

Our trips to America to perform music (as well as play football for charity!) were becoming more frequent. Travel had become such a big part of my life, not just on the roads of Ireland, but jumping on planes to different places. This was also a chance to see other countries and cultures, as well as meet up with peers and colleagues in the music industry. I loved absorbing all the new places and faces. I've always taken life in my stride in any case, and was happy to travel in whatever direction it took me, so I never felt overwhelmed or challenged by having to go to far corners of the world. Although sometimes it was exhausting, I really enjoyed it.

In 1977, we managed to take in some entertainment for ourselves when we were in New York City, which was always a real treat. The venue was Madison Square Gardens and the line-up was Chuck Berry and Fats Domino. Old-style rock'n'roll was still alive in New York at this time, despite the emergence of new genres like hard rock and disco, and to see so many people under one roof (16,000 at least) was quite a sight. The atmosphere was electric. The hospitality we received every time we visited the States was second to none, and I have always felt that the Irish have a certain place in the hearts of American people.

In November of that year, the pedigree of my excellent band and my top-class management came together, creating a week-long concert experience at the Gaiety Theatre in Dublin, called the Philomena Begley Country Jamboree Show. It was initiated by Eamonn Andrews of 'This Is Your Life' fame. He had approached Tony about doing a variety-style show where different artists would feature and be interviewed – a celebration of all things country, with me as the headliner. The Jamboree was an innovation in more ways than one, as it was also the first time in the theatre's 100-year history that a country music show was presented there. It was a completely new setting for me to perform in, and I suppose it was a gamble. None of us involved really knew what way it would go. But the loyal country fans turned up trumps, and made such a success of our Jamboree that the Full House signs had to go up. I was absolutely delighted, not only for myself, but also for my friends who took part. Working in the Gaiety was a wonderful experience. It's difficult to explain, but when you are up there on that stage performing, there's a certain feeling in your very bones that tells you when people are enjoying what you are doing. It's almost like a sixth sense, but for me it's every bit as real as my sight or hearing.

Of course, without my top-tier guests, the Jamboree would not have been the success that it was. Hank Locklin, who had flown in from America, was outstanding, but the Irish artists who had kindly accepted my invitation to take part proved that week that they too could stand up and be counted. Each night the Ramblin' Men and I were joined by Big Tom, Brian Coll, Ian Corrigan, Roly Daniels or Ray Lynam. Paschal Mooney, who compèred the show, also proved that he was one of the smoothest operators in the business. My week at the Gaiety was very hard work, but it was worth every minute of it.

Despite the busy lifestyle that my career was bringing my way, and the dizzy heights of success that brought me to so many exotic places and provided the most exciting opportunities, I was still very much 'a singing star by night, a mother by day'. I would commute daily to my showbiz bookings, regardless of the journey, regularly making a round trip of five hundred miles in one day. Mary was the apple of my eye, and the inspiration for many of my recordings with the Ramblin' Men, and during the day I was happiest pottering about with her as I did my household chores. That was home to me, and I was enjoying every moment of motherhood as well as being marvelled at for the magnificent way my career was going. Home was always important to me. It was a welcome haven from all the travelling, and the perfect balance to keep my feet firmly on the ground.

I did experience working-mother's guilt when I had to leave Mary, and she surely did know how to make me feel worse, as she'd cling to my leg and beg me not to go. I would drive away heartbroken, and would stop at the nearest phone box to check on her. I always got the same response:

'You wouldn't have reached the end of the lane when she stopped. She's happy as Larry now!' Dympna or Claire would tell me.

Mary had a lovely way of saying goodbye: she'd give me kisses to match the days until I'd get back. So if I was going to be away for two nights I'd get two kisses, three nights I'd get three and so on, but to be honest I tried to keep any long stays away from her to an absolute minimum. If a venue was within driving distance, I'd be home before she'd wake up, and I'd forgo sleep to make sure I had some time with her during the day.

As I settled into married life and motherhood, 1978 proved to be a crucial year for me. In the same twelve months that I lost my dear brother Patsy, the dream of all dreams came true: a night at the Grand Ole Opry. Life was hectic and our profile was increasing by the day, as we packed out dance halls and concert halls up and down the country, and soon we were booked to play in America again. The *first* time I sang at the Opry was in March 1978. The chance to perform at the Grand Ole Opry is probably the highlight of any country singer's career, and for me it was certainly no exception. In fact, in my case it was extra special, as I was the first Irish female artist to perform on that famous stage. Quite an achievement when you consider many American artistes have to wait years to make an Opry appearance.

On 14 March 1978, the Omagh-born country singer Brian Coll and I travelled to Nashville and New York, as part of a two-week trip to record in Nashville's top recording studio, Fireside Studios. We were guests of country singer and Grand Ole Opry member Hank Locklin, along with and Porter Wagoner, who had a string of top ten duet hits with Dolly Parton. Hank had toured Ireland in November the previous year with Brian and I, and with Tony, he decided to bring us over to America. He had set off home to Nashville with a copy of both of our albums in his suitcase! I don't think I really realised how significant it could be to have someone of his stature show enthusiasm for my work. To put him in perspective, Hank sold fifteen million records throughout his career, and his songs have been recorded by Dolly Parton, Willie Nelson, Dwight Yoakam and Dean Martin. His biggest hit, 'Please Help Me, I'm Falling', sold over one million copies alone!

Working with Hank and Porter was really the start of even greater things to come. In Europe and at home in Ireland, I was at the top of my game. I had hit a real high with the Country Jamboree at the Gaiety, which I really thought would be hard to top. Conquering America through the Nashville scene was something I could only ever have dreamed of. Yet now, within months, my records were off to Nashville in the suitcase of one of its most influential players.

Hank played my music to Porter Wagoner when he got back home, and Wagoner expressed amazement. He invited us over to record in Nashville the following March. He agreed to arrange and produce three albums – one each for Brian and I, and a third album of duets performed by the two of us. The Nashville team felt that if we recorded a duet, or better still, an album of duets, it had a good chance of making it big. But, alas, time ran out and we had to go home before we got to make it.

That first Nashville trip had begun with the St Patrick's Day parade, as guests of the Irish American Fifth Avenue Parade, and later we appeared at the Tower Ballroom, which was owned by an Irish man, Bill Hardigan. The following evening, 18 March, we set off for Nashville and the Grand Ole Opry, the Mecca of all country music and way beyond the reach of anyone but the very top country artists in the world. The venue was packed to capacity with 4,500 people, and it was breath-taking, to say the least, to have such an opportunity.

Nashville is home to many of the country world's best songwriters, of course. I learned while I was over there that Linda Hargrove, a songwriter who wrote one of my biggest hits, 'Once around the Dance Floor', had been trying to meet up with me, but unfortunately we didn't manage to get together because of our busy schedules. I still think that was such a pity. I'd love to have met her! I was absolutely gobsmacked to read what another famous songwriter in Nashville, Peggy Forman, had to say about my rendition of her big hit song, 'I'll Be a Lady Tonight':

'I am absolutely thrilled to hear that one of my songs has been recorded by an Irish artiste,' said Ms Forman in an interview with *Entertainment News*. 'This means much more to me than all my hits here in the States. I feel it's a great honour.'

Peggy's songs have been recorded by Conway Twitty and Connie Cato and she had a No. 1 hit with Loretta Lynn, so for her to even acknowledge my version of her song was outstanding.

The second time I went to Nashville was for the Opry's fifty-third birthday celebrations, on 21 October 1978. The night proved to be a double celebration, as Porter Wagoner announced to the crowd that it was also *my* birthday. The audience all joined the musicians on stage in singing a country version of 'Happy Birthday'. Quite a moment!

I received a surprise compliment from Justin Tubb (son of the famous Ernest), who also made an appearance that night. He thanked me for including one of his latest compositions, 'What's Wrong with the Way We're Doing It Now?', which I had done at Fireside Studios only hours before. It is still one of my most popular recordings.

With Roy Acuff, Minnie Pearl and Justin Tubb in Nashville for the Grand Ole Opry's fifty-third birthday celebrations in October 1978.

I was really knocked out by the way people treated me in Nashville on that second trip. Jeanne Pruett and I shared the same dressing room and she went out of her way to make sure that everything was okay for me. It was a very exciting time, and I was invited to tour with Porter Wagoner the following year, which proved to be a dream come true.

* * *

Nashville really is heaven for anyone who loves country music. I could also combine music with a bit of shopping during my downtime, you can imagine how much I was in my element!

One of my favourite outfits, that I still treasure, was bought in Nashville. When I first laid my eyes on it – a blue jumpsuit with studs, with a look of Elvis about it – I put it back on the railing when I saw the price. It was far too expensive. When I returned the following year, and visited the same boutique, I couldn't believe that this jumpsuit was still hanging there. It was fate, so I bought it and I've loved it ever since. If I could still fit into it I think I'd still wear it, I'm not joking! I remember being told that it would have to be cleaned in Los Angeles. Well, it came home with me to Galbally and I decided to 'Los Angeles' it myself, and it washed like a ribbon!

1978 was shaping up to be a turning point in my career. I was delighted to top the bill at major venues in Ireland, England and America, including the National Stadium in Dublin, the Ulster Hall in Belfast, the Royal Albert Hall in London and Carnegie Hall in New York. Four years into the Ramblin' Men, we had six silver discs and two gold discs. They were followed by many more, as advance sales before albums were even released were taken into account.

The soaring success of 1978 created massive milestones in my career, but this was tinged with great sadness with the loss of my darling brother Patsy. How proud he would have been to have followed my American adventures – no doubt he would have been on the phone to me every day for updates wherever in the world I was. I just wish he could have been there to experience such wonderful times.

* * *

Back in Ireland and a lot closer to home, a new support for musicians and performers was emerging in the shape of Downtown Radio, which had begun broadcasting from Newtownards, County Down, in 1976. For years, especially in the 1960s, national broadcasting authorities had been given a rude awakening by pirate radio stations. These stations were a lifeline to any unsigned or new artist starting out. By the mid-1970s, a network of locally based independent commercial radio stations had popped up across Ireland and the UK. In the North, Downtown Radio appeared just at the right time for me, during the swell of country music and the peak in my work with the Ramblin' Men.

I used to love going to Downtown for interviews, because I received exceptional friendliness and courtesy and I was always made to feel very special indeed. I'd arrive and before I knew I'd landed, I'd find myself chatting away on the air with a 'cuppa tay'. It felt like I was sitting in my own kitchen, having a good old yarn with friends. I formed lasting relationships with presenters such as Lynda Jane, Candy Devine and Big T.

When the Ramblin' Men hit their fifth year on the road, the Four Seasons Hotel in Monaghan was packed to capacity for a fantastic reception in our honour. We had just returned from the International Festival of Country Music at Wembley (which we were playing every year then), and on that same day, Hugh Hardy of Dundalk's Radio Carousel asked Boxcar Willie who had impressed him the most in London.

'Philomena Begley,' was his response. 'Because she displayed a feel and a love for the music and put it across in a most professional manner.'

I was asked a lot in those days why I thought country music was so popular. I always answered that it starts with the lyrics. The lyrics of a song, and the stories in country music, are truer to life and people readily identify with them. There is also a strong, simple beat to it – if you can't dance to country music, then you can't dance at all! And even at a dance, when people aren't paying as much attention as they would at a concert, I always try to chat between songs and find a connection in banter with the audience.

It was quite phenomenal how singers from the Ulster counties had such an influence on the country music scene as the 1970s came to a close. With the exception of a few, like Ray Lynam and Frank McCaffrey, all of the big Irish acts originated in Ulster and spread their music throughout the four provinces of the country. I used to joke that it was the fresh country air that was the secret to our success.

The secret to my success during this time was that I never really changed inside, despite everything that was going on around me. I remained myself and never tried to get above anyone else, a product, perhaps, of my solid

A promotional shot for 'The Umbrella Song', which appeared on my 1978 album, *Nashville Country*.

upbringing and the family values my parents instilled in me and my siblings. I wouldn't say it was my singing that brought me to the top, just being myself, really, and everything else fell into place. Success has never changed me one bit, and I do think being part of such a large family in rural Tyrone always made sure I kept my feet on the ground. When I would go home to the flick of the kettle and my family's every-day news, I knew I could never, ever get above myself.

When my album *Fireside Country* hit the charts in 1979, and my weekly show, 'Make Mine Country', presented with North Carolina country superstar George Hamilton IV, was being shown on BBC NI, I became known as the Queen of Country Music. It was a huge honour to receive this title, given the amount of talent on the road at the time.

On 28 September 1979, I played my last gig of that year and took a well-deserved break to give birth to my very own wee prince, Aidan. But when 1980 rolled in, it was back to work, as the dates and demands continued to come rolling in for Philomena Begley and Her Ramblin' Men. Busy, busy times indeed!

Chapter Twelve

The International Fame Game

It is true to say that Philomena Begley has now received from the Irish entertainment scene just about every award it has to offer. She has not been called the Irish Queen of Country Music for nothing. This being the case, it is natural that her future activities should include a considerable amount of work abroad.

Phil is of course no stranger to international audiences, having performed at Wembley on numerous occasions, recorded in Nashville and received the ultimate accolade in country music when she was invited to perform on two occasions on the Grand Ole Opry.

However, by no means does she intend to allow matters to rest there. She hopes to be back on the boards in January and begins right off with a major tour of Scotland where country music is beginning to break really big. This is immediately followed by an extensive tour of England. Both these tours are part of a promotional campaign being carried out by the major international record label K-Tel on Phil's album The Very Best of Philomena Begley [sic]. *Phil is the first Irish artiste to have been signed to K-Tel and her first album with them is being given the full treatment including a massive TV advertising campaign throughout the British Isles.*

In February she heads back to Nashville to record some more material with Porter Wagoner at Fireside Studios.

April sees her back at Wembley for yet another performance. Her slot will in fact be on 5th April and she appears on the same bill as Don Williams, The Bellamy Brothers, Tammy Wynette and a host of other country greats.

Wembley is of course a familiar place to Phil and she will no doubt put in another terrific performance but she breaks new ground with appearances at Frankfurt in Germany on March 30th and in Holland on Easter Sunday April 6th. Both of these now have become international country music festivals thanks to the efforts of promoter and country fan Mervyn Conn. Having built Wembley from virtually nothing into a massive event and made country music one of the most popular styles in Britain, Mr Conn is now doing exactly the same thing on the continent; it is significant that one of the major artistes that he has chosen to help him to this end is our own Phil Begley.

Entertainment News, October 1979

Even with three-year-old Mary, new baby Aidan and the busy farm life in Galbally with Tom, things on the work front showed no indication of slowing down. I was on the crest of a wave professionally by the time the

1980s came around. The international market was really opening up to me, and I had to rely on a lot of family support to keep it all going. I understand how difficult it is for any working mother in any business, but in the show business world, you have to strike when the iron is hot. Thankfully, I had the health and home base to let me embrace all that came my way.

By April 1980, the Ramblin' Men had been six years on the road. Another single, 'Blue Jean Country Queen', had topped the Irish country charts and was No. 1 on the playlist of Paschal Mooney's 'Keep it Country' radio show, broadcast twice weekly on RTÉ Radio Two. This track's popularity was being compared to my breakout hit, 'Blanket on the Ground'.

Meanwhile, my K-Tel album, *The Best of Philomena Begley*, had received a gold disc in Ireland. The TV campaign in Scotland prompted sales in the east and north of Scotland of almost 200 copies a day over many weeks.

Larry Cunningham, Joe Dolan, Brendan Harvey (K-Tel), Susan McCann and I celebrate in Dublin at the 1979 launch of my first record with K-Tel, *The Best of Philomena Begley*.

I spent another week in Nashville in April, with Porter Wagoner at Fireside Studios, where I recorded twenty-four songs, which would make up two albums. The material included a range of old standards plus some original numbers written for me especially by Porter Wagoner himself. Songs on this album included 'I'll Be the Lady Tonight', 'Let the Teardrops Fall on Me' and 'Mama's and Daddy's Little Girl'. I also had the pleasure of appearing on Porter's TV show, which was shown throughout the USA.

In May, I released the bouncy sounds of 'The Triangle Song'. It could soon be heard on the lips of children, milkmen and housewives throughout the country, and it went right to the top of the country music charts.

The best was yet to come for me that year, and it happened by way of a spectacular tour of Scotland in November, managed by a man named Bill Delaney. It started with two full-house shows in the Western Isles, and then we took Inverness by storm with another two sold-out shows. The excitement created by these appearances was hard to define or imagine. It was certainly new for me to be mobbed as if I was Mick Jagger, and it took me very much by surprise. The Scottish audiences were fantastic, and I loved every minute of entertaining. We finished at Aberdeen's Capitol Theatre, with an enormous reception from a capacity audience.

Towards the end of the year, following another successful festival at Wembley and a tour of Holland, I was invited to London, where I recorded a fifty-minute TV special called 'Christmas Holiday' with George Hamilton IV. The year of 1980 really was all go, from start to finish. On Gloria Hunniford's UTV show, I was presented with a platinum disc for over 50,000 Irish sales of *The Best of…* Gloria remarked that I was the first Irish country singer to gain platinum status for album sales.

And around that time, I discovered I was expecting my second daughter,

Carol. With three little ones at home, it became more difficult to manage my emotional and physical well-being. But singing was my job and I continued to juggle everything – not without hiccups, mind you.

When Carol was just eight months old, I drove down to Dublin for a gig, and the country was covered with a white blanket on the ground – snow! I pressed on, not realising that it would be one of the worst snowstorms the country had ever known. For three days, I was stuck in Dublin, worried and despairing. The country was in a panic, with everything at a standstill, but eventually I managed to make my way to the train station, where I caught a train to Dundalk. I was never so relieved to see Tom standing there, waiting to take me home to my family. Times like that really made me glad to switch off from the mad world of show business and spend time with the people who meant the most to me in the whole world. The guilt of a mother who has to leave her babies to work under any circumstances is always hard, but to be stuck somewhere like that was a frightening experience that I went through only the odd time.

In 1983, I was invited to represent Ireland at the European Gold Star Awards, which was, you could say, the country music equivalent of the Eurovision Song Contest. The awards were held in a lovely place called Tilburg, about an hour from Amsterdam, and there were over fifteen countries taking part. Rita Coolidge, the Grammy Award-winning singer and former wife of Kris Kristofferson, was special guest on the night, and it was televised all over Europe. I had brought a lovely white dress, but the producer told me they didn't like the colour white, and asked could I change into something else.

'Do you have another dress you could wear?' I was asked.

'Yes,' I replied.

'What colour is it?'

'White also,' I replied, and the producer's face fell. We were standing outside at the time, and Tom handed the dress over to me to show them, but it fell on the ground and became covered in mud, so it wasn't white any longer! Maggie Stapleton of RTÉ took charge and had the dress quickly washed and dried, and I went on stage wearing it despite the producer's reluctance.

I always subscribed to the saying, 'Where there's muck, there's money,' and it seemed to work for me, because I ended up coming home with the European Gold Star Award for Ireland! I have to say it was one of my proudest moments, taking that trophy home!

By now, I had toured England with country legends Glen Campbell, Charley Pride, Don Williams, T.R. Dallas and Foster and Allen. With Foster and Allen, we were away for about two weeks, and I offered to wash and iron their shirts which made me feel right at home! I used to joke on stage that I washed their shirts, but I had also come across a few pairs of smalls! We had a laugh a minute on that tour.

By 1984, Top Rank Entertainments was still flourishing and there were many new singers coming through. Maybe I was becoming one of the oldies, even though my diary was still quite full. Tony Loughman had done such an amazing job with the Ramblin' Men over the years, but sadly all good things have to come to an end, and our working relationship ended that year. I have always tried to embrace change rather than fear it; experience has shown me that change happens for a reason, and most of the time those reasons are for the best. I do remember Tony saying that, with so many big country stars now on his books, he thought I was coming to the end of the road. That was a hard thing to hear. Maybe I was stubborn

With Charley Pride at the National Concert Hall in Dublin.

and maybe I was just determined, but I didn't believe for one second that my career was over.

After creating the Ramblin' Men and then looking after us for ten years, as well as an international career and an award-winning run on home soil, Tony and I parted ways for reasons we always debated. Even though our versions of events differ, Tony and I were able to joke afterwards about the hows and the whys, about who sacked who! I took it on the chin. Our relationship was never tarred, and I worked with him again in later years.

Never one to rest on my laurels, I didn't waste any time after I left Top Rank. I quickly made my way to Ritz Records in Dublin, to Mick Clerkin, who had managed many of Ireland's showbands in the 1960s. I have never been able to keep still, and I'm always thinking of what is coming up next, so there was no way I was going to sit back and believe that all my hard work had dried up just like that.

I had recorded with Mick under his Release Records label with the

Country Flavour back in 1972. Mick had a long-term vision for country music following his experiences during the showband era. He would soon go on to discover a young man who had happened to come to me for advice around that same time in 1984.

I was up to my elbows in flour, baking bread at home one day, when an eager, dashing young man arrived in to see me. He was nervous, and was plucking at his jumper as he tried to tell me his plans and his hopes for the future; he wanted to be a singer. I think now that he caught me at a time when I was a bit disillusioned with the whole business, and was just really enjoying the moment at home, baking bread for my children. I was away from all the rushing and running about from venue to venue that the job demanded.

I wanted to be honest with him, so I stopped and thought for a while about what advice I could give him. And this is what I told him:

'Stick to the books.'

I remember his wee face fell, because it wasn't the encouragement or direction he was hoping to hear from me.

'Don't give up on a good old-fashioned education.'

Show business isn't an easy life, and so many people struggle to make a living from it, so I wasn't going to tell him it would be a bed of roses. There are a lot of elements of life on the road that the public just don't get to see, and I didn't want to build the lad's hopes up. I had seen so many ambitions fall apart over my twenty-plus years, and all I meant was for him to have a back-up plan, an education, in case his fate proved similar. I was concerned that if I filled his head with bright lights and big crowds and hit records, he would quote me if it didn't work out. Longevity (a word he later explained back to me!) is rare in show business. Without naming names, I'd already seen many eager young singers left disappointed when it all came crashing down around them. I guess you just never know how things will turn out. Thankfully, his passion and his talent meant that he can now quote me for trying to put him off the business. Even more thankfully, I am glad he didn't listen!

Because that wee lad was the one and only Daniel O'Donnell, and the rest, as they say, is country music history!

Chapter Thirteen

Shotgun and the Eighties

After the Ramblin' Men split up in 1984, I formed a band called Philomena Begley and Friends. Colm Keeley, Kevin McGinty and Kevin Farley of the Ramblin' Men stayed on with me, and this core was enhanced by Martin Cleary, John Gilmartin, Terry Duffy, Basil Hendrix, Don Woods and many more. We toured the circuit and carried on performing.

Meanwhile, Tom had decided to leave the music scene. Soon, each of the band members went their separate ways. Looking back, I can see now that Tom had clocked up a few more years on the road than I had, and he was happier to be at home on the farm with his cattle and, of course, our three children, Mary, Aidan and Carol.

The music scene had changed a lot, and our lives had become very fast –

Tom felt it was time to slow things down. He went full-time working with cattle – his first love – just as he had always done with his father. As he used to joke with us, 'At least the cows don't talk back.'

Being at home so much earned Tom a lot of respect from our children, and I am so proud of him for that. In a way, it was like parenting three different generations, as they all had very individual tastes and personalities. Mary was a wise wee soul and a bit old-school, you might say. Aidan was the lively one, and Carol was timid and quiet, but sharp enough in her own ways! You wouldn't pull the wool over her eyes, that's for sure! Having their daddy at home more definitely made life easier for them all, and it made sense to us, as I was still very much in demand. Tom and the children understood that. I couldn't give music up. I would have been very foolish if I ever had.

Tom made the children their breakfast every morning, and took them to school, and if I was away he'd make them dinner – his signature dish was good old bacon, cabbage and spuds! I was there most days, and as we had always agreed that they would never come home to an empty house, the new arrangement with their daddy around the farm worked very well as they moved through primary school.

My twentieth-fifth anniversary was in 1987. The BBC's 'Evening Extra', a TV news programme at the time, marked it with 'A Day in the Life', which included an appearance on a cold rainy night in Dublin as I played a gig with my new band, Shotgun. Shotgun had been formed in 1985 by a man called Charlie McBreen from Omagh, who managed artistes like Brendan Quinn. Later on, Sean McGrade took over as our manager with great success. Shotgun was Patsy Tweedy (drums) and Chris Blair (bass), both from Bangor, Liz Gordon from Dromara (piano) and Stephen

Collecting my British Country Music Association Award in 1985.

Smyth from Portaferry (steel and lead guitar). When Chris left, Seamus Rooney from Portaferry stepped in. In the 'Evening Extra' episode, I was all decked out in an orange trouser suit, with tall white boots over the trousers, topped off with a good old eighties permed 'mullet' hairstyle.

It was a welcome change for me to have another female in my band, and Liz and I got on like a house on fire. We had many laughs. When we played in London, we'd go to Paddington Station and spend our days people-watching until it was time to perform. On stage with the late greats Glen Campbell and Don Williams, we had a real rapport. She was one of the finest keyboard players in the country, and it was nice to have someone to fall out with over hairspray, and who took up the most space in the hotel room! Thanks Liz!

Once, on our way to the Silkeborg Country Festival in Denmark, we were held up at the airport and we missed our flight because one of the lads couldn't find his passport. As we were waiting for the next plane, we got chatting to a man called Stéphane Grappelli. I had no idea he was the very famous French jazz violinist. Patsy Tweedy asked him to play a tune, which he did, and I joined him in a version of 'Forty Shades of Green'!

Away from touring with Shotgun, my typical day in the 1980s started at 8.30am, when I'd get the children out to school. In the evening, after having dinner with them and depending on where I was playing that night, come rain, hail or snow, I'd be off to my next engagement for a two-hour show, which might finish as late as 2am. Some nights, I wasn't home until four or five in the morning. I felt the most energetic when I came off stage at that time of night. As the saying goes, I could have driven to Cork, such was the high I felt from the buzz of being on stage and the energy from the audience, who danced as I sang into the wee hours.

I had a hectic schedule at home and abroad, but, even though I was probably exhausted, I never had time to think about it. I just kept going. Truth be told, it was adrenaline and a pure passion for entertaining and singing that kept me going, and I felt on top of the world when I was out on the road with the band.

So, when the presenter of 'Evening Extra' asked why I still persisted with such a lifestyle, I explained that it was my life, and without it I didn't know what I would do. I was more softly spoken in media interviews then – looking back, I can see how I have grown more confident and more comfortable in front of the camera since. On stage, I had developed a persona – a jokey, confident performer who could interact with an audience I'd known for a quarter of a century – but when it came to speaking to journalists on a one-to-one basis, often with a camera pointed in my face, I never ceased to feel daunted!

I liked to stick close to my roots, no matter how much in demand I was. The truth is, behind the glitz and glamour, I had a wee inferiority complex. Yes, I had wealth and a nice existence, paid for by my years of hard work, but still I wondered what others thought. I think, too, that I was juggling it all to prove that I really was no different to anyone else, that inside I hadn't changed at all. I didn't want to even try to live up to the image of being a big star. I was just happy doing what I was doing, and I tried not to analyse it too much, for fear of becoming even more in wonder of it all. I felt insecure when meeting important people or when being interviewed by the media, but I just didn't feel any different inside. Much of the showbiz lifestyle just didn't seem real to me. Don't get me wrong – with the right company, I love to let my hair down as much as anyone else, but mingling for too long in so-called celebrity circles or going off the rails never was of interest to me. Mind you, my pioneer days ended in the 1980s and I learned how to party like the rest of them very soon after.

I think that a lot of my insecurities came from my lack of a formal education. Remember, I left school at fifteen to work in the hat factory, and I never looked back. Sometimes I knew exactly what I wanted to say, but I often found it hard to find the words to express my opinion of the industry I was immersed in. There was often a perception that country music was simply all fringes and frills and horses and hats, but I knew different of course – country music in the 1980s was big business!

What I would have wanted to say to any critics of country music is that I had been absorbed in the industry from its very beginnings. I had seen the transformation of many céilí bands, such as our very own Old Cross, and I had gone on to be recognised for commercial hits with the Country Flavour. Through the heyday of the Ramblin' Men, and my solo successes in the UK and the US, what had begun as an innocent passion – and maybe even a lucky accident, as I'd never set out to be a performer – was now a very serious business for me and those who depended on me. And although I have never been ruled by materialistic ways, we all need to earn a living. I had simply found a way that worked for me and my family.

A publicity shot from the 1980s.

Meanwhile, back to the 1980s! The Troubles in Northern Ireland were still rife, but despite the heart-breaking destruction, we always tried to keep everyday life light-hearted. The UTV presenter Gloria Hunniford recently told me the story of the time she was sent from the bright lights of Belfast to the rolling fields of Galbally to give me an award, and how the results were hilarious.

'Philomena Begley was at the height of her country music success when I was asked to present her with a gold disc award live on TV, as part of Ulster Television's "Good Evening Ulster" programme,' recalls Gloria. 'We ventured with our small crew to her home and farm in County

Tyrone, and the director of the programme, Brian Woodell, came up with the crazy notion that the grand presentation should be done when we were both on horseback! Now, this seemed like a clever idea at the time, but there was only one problem, and that problem to me was a very big one ... I hadn't been on a horse in my life apart from maybe the odd pony trek, and I hadn't the first clue of what I was doing! I still can't believe that we actually got away with it!

'I was with Ulster Television from 1969 until 1982, so all during the Troubles the news slots were filled with what we called "bullets, bombs and barricades", and our viewers were really in need of some light relief from the hard-line news that was being transmitted into their homes on a daily basis. So "Good Evening Ulster" took on the challenge, under the vision of Brian, to put out a one-hour live show every evening which would be entertaining around the news, and show that life did indeed go on around the Troubles. It was a very brave thing to do considering what was going on but people loved to see what big stars like Philomena Begley were getting up to. Philomena was a very big player, and I interviewed her a lot down the years. She was always a good chat, full of enthusiasm and pleasant, so when the quirky idea of our paths crossing and a gold disc being presented on horseback, we knew there was no better woman, and it worked a treat! I'm sure the UTV archives have it somewhere!'

It was in June 1985 that I was honoured to meet the wonderful Tammy Wynette. She brought me to her home – the famous First Lady Acres, which her husband George Jones had bought for her in Nashville. Tammy was a fabulous host and she took a lot of time in showing me around, including a look at her outstanding trophy and gold disc collection. The best thing I remember about her house is that it had twelve bedrooms! I had lots of time for Tammy, and was so sad to hear of her passing so young, at the age of just fifty-five in 1998.

My connection with Tammy does not end there though. After her death, I embarked on a tour with her daughter, Georgette Jones, when she came to Ireland to pay tribute to her mother, and I introduced her to a steel guitar player called Jamie Lennon. Well, I must have a bit of the old Cupid touch, because they went on to marry in 2011! I think I could be an excellent matchmaker, actually. I have had many couples tell me they met at my shows and dances, and lots of people saying their parents met when listening to me sing back in the early days. So you never know, I could be a dating expert if it ever goes all wrong.

As the new millennium fast approached, my career as a country singer was still keeping my diary full. The matchmaking world would just have to wait for me another wee while!

Chapter Fourteen

New Millennium, New Adventures

After Shotgun ended, and with the 1990s upon us, I found myself able to be more selective about where and when I sang and performed, but I still never stopped and, thankfully, was still in demand. I suppose you could say I became more 'freelance' around this time, having left the commitment of a regular band behind and being able to pick and choose what shows I wanted to take part in. I rarely said no to anything, however, as I always felt it a privilege to be asked in the first place. I still find it very hard to say no!

My adventures on the road as a solo artist were colourful and plentiful, and I have lots of them to recollect and many, many stories to tell from off the stage too.

Left: Recording with Margo in Nashville, 1996.

Below: Daniel O'Donnell presenting me with the infamous Tyrone Crystal Crown for my thirtieth anniversary in show business, 1992.

Left: With the legendary Tammy Wynette in her garden at First Lady Acres, Nashville, in 1985.

Below: Holidaying with Tom on the slopes in France in the early 1990s.

Back home in The Diamond in Pomeroy for a charity tandem bike ride. Behind me stands Pat Cush (née Quinn), mother of Malachi Cush. Beside me is my very old friend Josie McKernan.

Album covers through the years.

Right: Showing off a snazzy outfit in the 1990s.

Below: With the Queens – Jeannie Seely, Louise Morrissey, Dee Reilly and Billie Jo Spears – on tour in 2009.

Above: One of the last photos taken of Billie Jo and me on stage in the Waterfront Hall in 2011.

Below: With Big T of Downtown Radio.

Right: With Nathan Carter, who claims I was the first singer to ask him up on stage to perform.

Below: 50 Years of Music and Memories – with my guests Daniel O'Donnell, Andrea Begley, Aidan Quinn and Ray Lynam.

Above: The Begley clan in more recent times. Clockwise from top left: my cousin Mary Quinn, my brother Plunkett, my sister Margaret, my brother Kieran, my sister Angela, myself, my sister Mary and my sister Annette.

Right: On stage at my 50 Years of Music and Memories concert.

In May 1990, I was very honoured to take part in a tour with two of America's greatest country stars, Glen Campbell and Don Williams. Glen was such a gentleman – he would come backstage and into the dressing rooms and make sure to say hello before every performance. Don Williams was a quieter sort. He would keep himself to himself, not wanting to intrude on anyone's company, but he was always very polite and professional as we toured around the UK.

The following year, Mick Flavin approached me about working together and out of that conversation came our album of duets, *In Harmony*. We went on a hugely successful tour of Ireland and Scotland, with full houses almost every night.

In 1992, I marked thirty years on the road with that wonderful celebration in Dublin, when Daniel presented me with the infamous crystal crown. In November the same year, I received one of my most significant accolades, at the British Country Music Association Awards, for my contribution to the development of country music in Britain. In June 1995, I was invited to attend Nashville's Fan Fair, where country artists gather for a week and perform concerts which are geared towards meeting fans from all over the world.

Performing at the Silkeborg Country Festival in Denmark in 1993.

My worldly travels continued, and in 1996, I recorded an album of duets with Margo O'Donnell in Nashville. We sang songs such as 'Golden Memories', 'Husband Hunting' and 'The Way Old Friends Do'. Margo and I go back a long, long way. It was always a pleasure to work with and tour with her, as she'd been on the road for almost as long as I had.

* * *

One of my frequent 'haunts' – pardon the pun – when I visited Birmingham during the late 1990s, was a hotel called the Old Crown. The building dates from the fourteenth century, and it is world famous for being haunted! The first time I stayed there, the band dropped me off, and I was delighted to be accommodated in the finest bedroom, complete with a big four-poster bed and a fancy bathroom. I had no idea there was a history to the hotel, but I would soon find out for myself. Later that night, as I lay there trying to get to sleep, I had an awful feeling that there was someone else in the room. If I'd had a few drinks in me, I probably wouldn't have noticed, but I was stone cold sober. It felt like there was someone under the bed, pushing it up in the middle, so I got down on my hands and knees and looked underneath. Of course there was nothing to be seen. This went on the whole night, and I barely slept a wink. I thought it must have been my overactive imagination, so I put it to the back of my mind.

The second time I stayed there was in 2002, along with Ann McAvoy, our tour manager, and her brothers Gary (a singer in the band I was on tour with) and Keith (their sound man). Susan McCann and her husband Dennis were on the same tour. When we called it a night, Ann and I went to the room we were sharing. She slept in the big fancy bed, while I lay on a wee single bed across from her. I was trying to learn a song at the time called 'If You've Got Leaving on Your Mind', so I was lying down with my earphones in and my eyes closed. I was in a world of my own, when Ann pounced out of the bed and ran over to me in an awful panic.

'Philly! Wake up! Wake up!' she said. 'Someone or something keeps pulling the blankets off me!'

I jumped up, not knowing what on earth was going on. When she told me again, we both ran out of the room and down the corridor to wake everybody. Gary had no sympathy whatsoever.

'Go back to your room and turn on the lights,' he said. 'I don't believe in that oul' craic!'

So we did, but we barely slept a wink, as the fear of God was in us. I had definitely felt something strange about the room the last time I was there, and now Ann did too.

Susan and Dennis were up early the next morning, and we went into their room to tell them what happened. Susan was wide-eyed and she totally believed us, as she had had some spooky goings on too.

'The kettle in our room kept switching on and off, all by itself, all night,' she told us.

Of course, the boys from the band then proceeded to exaggerate. They joked about towels jumping off rails and other such nonsense, but when we were checking out, we saw there was a big book full of ghost stories about the rooms we had stayed in. We were asked to fill out our own experiences. So we're sure we weren't making it up.

When Billy Morrissey, who runs Country Music Holidays, invited me to go to Newfoundland, Canada, in 2009, to tour with Louise Morrissey and Sandy Kelly, I was more than delighted to take part. It was fabulous to see that part of the world. On our way home, Matt McGrenaghan, the Donegal fiddle player who was also on tour with us, drove my car from Shannon to Bundoran. We thought we'd clipped the jetlag by sleeping on the plane, so I can't say that I was too tired when I took over the wheel to make my way home to Tyrone. I drove along a route I was very familiar with – roads that I knew like the back of my hand – and I didn't really feel as though my eyes were dropping. But when I was about three miles from home, I fell asleep for a split second and crashed my car into a post, and then proceeded to take out six more wooden posts along the side of the road before the car eventually came to a stop. I woke up with the impact of the blows, and when I saw what I thought was smoke filling the car, I got out immediately and stood in the field. But then I realised that I had left my mobile phone in the car, and I would need it to call for help. I was terrified as I made my way back to the car, worried that if it would blow up at any moment but it turned out that the smoke was actually dust from the airbag. Although the car was severely damaged, I was very lucky to escape unmarked, something I am grateful for to this day.

I rang home immediately, and Aidan and Tom came to rescue me as quickly as they could, relieved that I was alive to tell the tale.

* * *

Being asked to take part in any TV show is always a big honour for me. As the years passed by, some of the requests that came in were becoming more and more adventurous and obscure, to say the least, but none more so than my appearance in 2008 on the hilarious 'Podge and Rodge Show' on RTÉ Two. Podge and Rodge were two very cheeky red-haired puppets, who got up to all sorts of antics with their celebrity guests. Their humour could be very adult, and was sometimes very close to the bone. They asked me to dress up as the late Amy Winehouse, in an orange satin dress, and perform one of her biggest hits, 'Rehab'. Needless to say, I laughed the whole way through it, especially in make-up, when I was given a beehive wig and several tattoos, including one across my chest that read 'Blake'. Amy's signature heavy eyeliner was a fine job to get on, and I'd even more of a handling trying to get it off. The transfer tattoos especially didn't seem to want to come off, and I was stuck with them for days! I even tried nail polish remover on them. The whole thing was half-mad from start to finish, so I wasn't surprised to be in a spot of bother after it. I enjoyed it immensely though, and when I looked back at the capers of some of the other guests, I realised that I had probably got off lightly!

It's lovely to have such things to laugh about. The world of television really opens up so many opportunities for people in this business. Just such a thing happened for a very close relative of mine in 2013, when she was the overall winner of the then BBC TV talent series 'The Voice UK'.

My niece Andrea Begley is the daughter of my youngest brother, Kieran, and for as long as I can remember, Andrea just loved to sing. All our family gatherings were filled with music and from when she was a young child, Andrea's party piece was usually a Mary Black song. I used to call her up on stage too when she was a little girl, which she seemed to love. So I wasn't very surprised when she entered 'The Voice UK' on BBC One, and made the grand final under the guidance of her mentor, The Script's Danny O'Donoghue.

On stage in the 1980s with my niece Andrea Begley, who went on to win 'The Voice UK' in 2013.

I travelled to London to see her in the final, and to say it was nerve-wracking is an understatement. Andrea had big competition on the night – will.i.am seemed to favour the other finalist, Leah McFall from Belfast, and we all knew it could go either way when so many factors, not least nerves, could affect either girl's performance. But Andrea did so well, singing a really moving rendition of Sarah McLachlan's 'Angel' and a beautiful version of 'My Immortal' by Evanescence. It was still unbelievable when her name was called out as the winner. I will never forget Andrea's mother's face. She was in complete shock.

'Ann, she won!' I called over to her, but poor Ann was in a complete daze. It really was a remarkable achievement, and we were all as proud as punch.

I remember I couldn't figure out will.i.am, as he seemed to be on his phone constantly, but I later found out he was tweeting live updates about the show, which is completely out of my experience! What would I know about tweeting? I thought he was just being rude, fiddling with his phone while the contestants were singing their hearts out and trying their best! All of the judges were very nice though, and we were all excited to meet will.i.am, Jessie J. and Danny O'Donoghue. But the one I was looking forward to meeting the most was the one and only Sir Tom Jones ... Would I get to meet him in the flesh? I certainly hoped so!

I had borrowed a camera in Dublin from my friend Kathleen Cahill, who had left me off at the airport, and I got some fantastic pictures of all the contestants and the whole team. And just as I'd hoped to, I got chatting to Mr Jones himself. I told him about the song 'Elusive Dreams', and he began to sing it with me, which was a moment I will never forget. I was on top of the world. Imagine getting to sing with Sir Tom Jones!

We went to an after party and again, there were more photo opportunities but, alas, when I got up the next morning, my camera was nowhere to be found. I still to this day can't figure out where it got to, or who might have taken it. I was so gutted to have lost my precious record of a very proud night for all of my family.

There was big excitement in Pomeroy, and a grand homecoming was planned for Andrea in the days after her big win. Thankfully she is still keeping busy and singing a lot – we keep promising to do some work together, so we'll have to get a move on and get something organised soon!

I remember meeting Storm Keating, wife of Boyzone singer Ronan Keating, who was part of the production team on The Voice. She came over to me that night to tell me that Ronan said hello. This made me smile, as I have fond memories of Boyzone's very first television appearance on RTÉ's 'The Late Late Show' in 1993, when I was a guest too. They were just young lads at the time, and my good old friend Louis Walsh, who I had known for many years, brought them along to make their big television debut. The boys had no songs prepared, though, so they just danced along to some music and Gay Byrne, the then host, famously asked the audience if they thought the boys would make it big. They had sold 25 million records by 2013, so I think it's fair to say that they have!

I chatted to them in the Green Room after their performance that night, and I have to say they were all very endearing.

'Don't forget me when you're famous,' I told them, and they all laughed and carried on. Then I gave them a wee bit of advice using the words of a song by Jean Shepard:

'Be nice to everybody on your way up; you're going to meet 'em again coming down.'

I didn't see the boys again for many years, but one evening I was at the Big Buzz Awards in Belfast and I met Keith Duffy. He was there as part of the cast of 'Coronation Street', which he had joined in the years after Boyzone. I also saw Shane Lynch, Uri Geller and many soap and media personalities.

'You probably don't remember me,' I said. 'But I remember chatting to you many years ago, when you made your first TV appearance in Ireland.'

Keith gave me a smile and a nod, and he said:

'I remember you surely, and I also remember the advice you gave us. In fact, we chatted about it many times down the years.'

He called Uri Geller over to tell him what I'd said to them, and when Keith went on stage to pick up his own award, he told the same story to the audience. I was there to pick up an award on behalf of Snow Patrol, and I sang 'The Way Old Friends Do', for which the audience got their lighters out. It is an evening I will always remember fondly.

* * *

No matter how many people from the music or show business world I meet, I never really get star-struck – in fact, half of the time this is because I don't know who they are! I sat with Chris Rea for ages one night at a recording of 'The Late Late Show', and I had no idea who he was! At the end of the day, I think of us as just people doing a job, so there's no point in getting too excited!

I enjoy working in television, whether it's as a chat show guest, a singer or a presenter, like back in 1979, when I got to work with George Hamilton IV, co-presenting a special six-week spin-off of the BBC NI programme 'Make Mine Country'. A few well-known American stars, such as the Browns, came across to be on the show, and we profiled lots of Irish singers too: Brendan Quinn, the late fiddler Paddy O'Flaherty (who also presented 'Make Mine Country') and Susan McCann. George had always been very good to us when we visited Nashville in the early days, even taking me to meet Skeeter Davis and organising fun nights out for us, so it was nice to be able to show him some Irish hospitality in return.

I do like meeting new people from all walks of life, as well as going to nice places in the name of 'work'. Mickey Magill, who runs an entertainments agency in Northern Ireland, often organises cruise-ship concerts, and he invites some of Ireland's top country stars to entertain holidaymakers over a period of about a week. I have participated in many of these trips, but one of the most memorable travelled across the Bay of Biscay, off the north coast of Spain. Its famous stormy weather and its geography are troublesome for ships and their crews, and it is said that sailors fear it because there have been many shipwrecks. There were many big names on that cruise, including Susan McCann, the comedian Conal Gallen, Malachi Cush and lots more, and every single one of us was seasick as the ship battled through the choppiest of waters and into a big storm. I had to sit on a chair with stabilisers on it, because everything on the ship was moving around. It was like something you'd see in a movie!

Luckily, the artistes on the cruise were all professionals, and had a bit of craic about them. So, although the weather was absolutely awful, we still ended up having fun and enjoying ourselves – as the old saying goes, 'It was that bad, it was good'! Most package tours are easier than this, especially around mainland Europe and Spain, and my fellow artistes and I will more often spend our days in the sun and our nights entertaining our fans from all over the UK and Ireland. Show business can put many hurdles in your way, but in country music we like to make sure the punters have a good time, no matter what the elements might ask of us!

Chapter Fifteen

2012:

Fifty Years in

Show Business

The year 2012 was always going to be a significant one for me. To think that by then, I had clocked up fifty years in show business! From that first night when I stood on the stage, as a wee slip of a girl who worked in a factory, I went on to travel the world with my music, playing on the greatest stages I could ever have imagined and meeting the most wonderful people along the way.

Aidan really wanted to mark this milestone with a good old celebration, one that would last as long as it possibly could. We decided to bring it back to where it all began, at Ardboe Hall on the shores of Lough Neagh, County Tyrone. I returned there to play on 12 May 2012, and it was a magical and emotional night, as I thought of all that had happened in the intervening years: the days of the Old Cross Céilí Band, the massive popularity of the Country Flavour, the heyday of the Ramblin' Men, the 1980s and early 1990s with Shotgun, the tours and the trips to Nashville, and all the beautiful friendships that formed along the way.

I was over the moon to see so much interest from everyone who joined in the celebrations of that jubilee year. It was an action-packed year, which included the release of a three-CD set of greatest hits called *From Then to Now*, and a dance hall tour throughout Ireland and the UK that took me around many venues from May to August.

In September, we headed to the sun for a party in the Sol Principe Hotel on the Costa del Sol. I was joined by a host of stars, including Foster and Allen, Daniel O'Donnell, Susan McCann, Ray Lynam, Eamon McCann, Frank McCaffrey, former Ramblin' Man Francie Smith and DJ Big O, to name just a few. To say we had a ball is an understatement. It was billed as the showbiz event of the year, and I have to say we weren't disappointed.

Another highlight of the year occurred at the Greenvale Hotel in Tyrone. I was joined once again by friends and family, at another 'This Is Your Life'-type event, hosted by Kerry GAA legend Mick O'Dwyer. I had links with Mick via the Top Rank Superstars football matches in Ireland and America in the 1970s.

Once again, it was a very emotional evening for me, as my own brothers and sisters each took the mic and told memories and Begley family tales. A tear came to my eye as I thought of my parents and our brother Patsy. Our father had died in 1998, aged eighty-three, and we had only just lost our mother in 2012, at the age of ninety-eight. How proud they would have been, but I know they were looking down on us all and joining in the craic from up above.

Mick was a fine host, and he introduced a range of speakers, including the man who guided my career for many years, Tony Loughman. I have to say my years under his management are filled with many fond memories. Tony has since sadly passed away, but I love that I still bump into his wife and children for a catch-up.

My fellow Tyrone singer and lifetime friend, Brian Coll, told a few stories, as did another Tyrone great, the late Gene Stuart, who again I was very honoured to have worked with down the years. The Tyrone boys were out in force that night, and it just shows what our county has contributed to country music. I was reminded of the challenges and hurdles we faced as we continued to bring music to Irish people throughout thirty years of the Troubles. It made me so proud to be from Tyrone *and* to still be singing.

The line-up was completed with the wee man from Strabane, singer and BBC Radio Ulster host Hugo Duncan, who joined in and reminisced on some of the good times.

The showband era was represented by my neighbour from Armagh, John Glenn, who was famous for fronting the Mainliners during the 1960s, and we even had a few footballers along – County Down's James McCartan and Paddy Doherty, and Donegal's Brian McEniff. My good friend and our ardent supporter, Fr Brian D'Arcy, gave a touching and hilarious speech. And I was even presented with a 'big red book', which is my pride and joy. It includes lots of photos and memories from those fifty years – truly something to treasure. I am so appreciative of everyone who took the time to come along on the night, as well as those who made such an effort in the organisation of it all. It was something else, I can tell you, and I still get a warm feeling inside when I think of that night.

The celebrations didn't get in the way of the workload though, as I recorded a new album, *How I Love Them Old Songs*, in the autumn of 2012. It was my first release of new material in ten years, so it was a very exciting project to work on. This was followed by a DVD celebrating fifty years, which was presented by my cousin Pat's son, Malachi Cush, and directed by my son, Aidan. Isn't it nice to have so many talented young ones in the family?!

I even got my running shoes on that year. Believe me, they had seen better days, but I managed to take part in the Belfast City Marathon, where I helped to raise some funds for the MRI Scanner Appeal for the Royal Belfast Hospital for Sick Children. It was a big challenge for me, but an absolute delight to be able to do something nice for others to mark my own fifty years.

Throughout the year, I enjoyed a lot of media coverage, and I have to say, the press and broadcasters of Ireland were very enthusiastic and supportive. TG4 produced a Christmas special, the station's most viewed programme that year, which brought a very memorable twelve months to a close.

It was at this time that I really did look back and reflect on how far I'd come. I am still mesmerised at how totally supportive my friends, family and peers have been. A lot of those people took time to send me a few words of congratulations, and I'm delighted to share them with you here.

PETER AIKEN

Philomena Begley recorded her first single, 'Come, Me Little Son', on my father, Jim Aiken's, Dolphin Label. My father presented her with her very first disc on behalf of the label at the Starlight Ballroom in Belfast. Aiken Promotions have been delighted to work with Philomena over the years, she has been a great ambassador for country music during her fifty-five years in the business and we hope to work with her for many more.

TONY ALLEN

Philomena is one of the few singers who can take a song and make it her own – she has stamped her trademark vocals on great ballads and dance floor hits alike. Listening to Philomena singing reminds me that she has nothing to prove – she's done it all. Wishing you many more happy anniversaries.

JIMMY BUCKLEY

Philomena is a larger-than-life character on and off stage. In my humble opinion, there has never been another lady who can sing country songs the way she can sing them here in Ireland. No one has come along in all those years to fill her boots. She's fantastic and I wish her all the very best. Just brilliant!

NATHAN CARTER

Congratulations Philomena – I will never forget the night you asked me to sing a song at a concert in the Abbey Hotel, Donegal, just over four years ago. Since that memorable night, we have shared many stages together and I know that you have always taken a keen interest in my career – and just like a fine wine, your voice is maturing with age. You are a real lady, a star and a true friend. I wish you all the best on your fiftieth year on the road, and may that road never end.

MALACHI CUSH

I've always been aware of Philomena throughout my life. This larger-than-life personality is a first cousin of my mother's and there has always been a great closeness between our two families. As a young lad I remember going to see one of Philomena's concerts. I used to call her Aunty Philly because I always thought that gave me a little more prestige and made me feel a little bit more important! That night I went to see her, I got a big mention from the stage and I was proud as punch. I have developed a great friendship with her son Aidan and I used to go up to their home in Galbally during my summer holidays. It was all of five miles up the road from my own home but it felt like a different world altogether, just like Philomena used to feel when she spent her early childhood on holidays at Gortnagarn where my own mother, her cousin Pat Quinn, lived. Philomena radiates a warmth that makes you feel so important and she does that with everyone she meets. She is certainly someone I will always look up to in the music industry. For all of the great memories you have given to me and my family, Philomena, I thank you. For all of the great memories you still have to give us in future, I thank you for those too. I wish you every happiness in your celebrations of this very impressive and important milestone.

FR BRIAN D'ARCY

Philomena revels in being an ordinary woman who is a wife, mother, grandmother, but once the band strikes the chord, she sings with as much enthusiasm and enjoyment as she did when she sang all those years ago with the Old Cross Céilí Band. I have been around many a corner with Philomena. We've helped each other at weddings and funerals. I've enjoyed her company in bars and ballrooms. I've enjoyed her yarns and stories, her jokes and tall tales, her insights into other artists, her fanaticism about Tyrone football and her enduring charity to those in need. She sings 'How Great Thou Art' with hymnal fervour and then regales us with stories about 'Blanket on the Ground' with just the right amount of bawdiness.

Philomena is one of those people who you love to meet. She gives herself totally to everything and at the end of the show when we mere mortals are ready to go home, Philomena is ready to party. I think that she will go on forever.

MIKE DENVER

What can I say about Philomena that hasn't been said before? She's a gifted entertainer, one of a kind. Philomena has been part of our nationwide concert tour for the past two years and as we travelled all over Ireland, the stories that she has shared from her fifty years on the road are amazing, for as well as being a great singer, she is always craic. I save her number on my mobile phone as 'The Queen', so that I am reminded that when I am speaking to her I am speaking to country music royalty. Philomena, it's an honour to work with you. You're a gem.

HUGO DUNCAN

Philomena has been a friend of mine for many a long day and even before I joined the music business professionally, she has always been a lady I admired as an artist. It is great when you meet somebody you admire and you find out that they are just as nice as you had hoped they would be. Not only is Philomena a fantastic singer and performer but she is also a fantastic person – a person whose company you love being in. Long may she reign as she *is* the Queen of Country Music.

MICKEY HARTE

Philomena, I'm delighted to share a little bit of reflection on your long, long career in the showbiz world. You're such an example to us all, because as the years have gone on you just keep getting better and better. When we've come home over the last number of years with Sam Maguire, which we have been lucky enough to do on numerous occasions, it always felt you were really home when you saw Philomena up on the stage with Cuthbert Donnelly and her battering out the music. It was you of course, Philomena, doing the singing and Cuthbert helping you along with a few hand claps! We often heard the lilts of 'The Mountains of Pomeroy' and that told us we were home, especially to me as my father came from the same village as you did. You're such a live and enthusiastic person, always good to be around for a bit of craic and a bit of banter. I'm just delighted to be able to share how special you are not only to those who love country music, but to the people of Tyrone because you are a Tyrone woman, and that's what makes us proud of you the most.

MARGO

What I have to say about Philomena would take about three or four big books, to tell some of the fabulous times we have had together. I've known her since she was with the Old Cross and you know, there is only one Queen and that's Philomena. Not only is she a great singer, but she is one of my favourite people and I love her to bits. Happy fiftieth Philomena! I love you loads!

IVAN MARTIN

I first met Philomena Begley in 1977 at the Ideal Home Exhibition in the King's Hall, Belfast. Her albums were flying out the door of Sounds Around (a record shop I had – remember those?!) and we were both exhibiting at the exhibition. She came over for a chat and we have been gabbing away ever since. The big song for Philly at that time was 'Blanket on the Ground' and we could have done with one of those about four years ago when we met on a flight to London. Somebody spilled a cup of tea over Philomena during the flight and her denim suit was soaked through. When we landed, my wife Suzanne went into the ladies' to help the Queen to dry off and change. To her surprise, Philly's suitcase was packed with CDs and DVDs, but no change of clothes. 'I'm off to play at a festival in Denmark,' she explained. 'I thought it would pass the afternoon if I went shopping there for an outfit for the gig.' This just proves that there are three reasons why Philly is at the top for so long: 1. She knows the important things to pack when travelling; 2. She has an enduring talent and; 3. She has never lost the run of herself and audiences everywhere love her for it. Good luck, Philly – keep doing what you're doing!

SUSAN McCANN

It was Philomena who showed me the way up – how girls from rural Ireland could head up their own bands, record albums, headline stage and TV shows and travel the world. Congratulations Philly on fifty years and I wish you plenty more!

DANIEL O'DONNELL

I grew up with Philomena's music and I've always been a big fan of this wonderful singer. Philomena was a great inspiration to me, along with my sister Margaret (Margo) when I decided to follow my own path in music. It's not an easy life because so many people struggle to make a living out of it, and I remember that day in 1984 going to her home and asking for advice and seeing her up to her elbows in flour, baking bread – you see, we all lead normal lives away from the stage. However, I had a passion for what I was doing and no matter what anyone said to me I was determined to give it a go and I've been so lucky that it has all worked out for me. I will always respect Philomena's concern for me and she will always be my No. 1 female singer. Congratulations Philomena on fifty years in show business. You are a wonderful ambassador both at home and abroad and it's a real thrill for me to be part of your celebratory tour.

CHARLEY PRIDE

I first met Philomena back in the 1980s at the Wembley shows. Since then, we have performed all over Ireland and the UK on tours promoted by the late Jim Aiken and the late Tony Loughman. I remember I caught a glimpse of her in the crowd at a Fan Fair in Nashville, and that gave me the opportunity to bring her up to the podium and introduce her to the crowds there. The last time we caught up was on 'The Late Late Show' in 2017, and, you know, she hasn't changed a bit. I'm glad to call her my friend.

DEREK RYAN

Philomena is one of the most inspirational and iconic singers in Ireland. After fifty years in the business she is still the same kind person who is always on hand to offer support to new and up and coming artists. Happy anniversary Philomena – I wish you many more years of success and hits.

ROGER RYAN

I've had the privilege of knowing Philomena Begley as an artist and a friend for most of her professional career. Over the years we have been involved in many promotions together and I have always found her to be a true professional in everything she does.

Blessed with a great natural talent, she also possesses the ability to really communicate with people, both on and off the stage. She is without doubt, one of the finest performers this country has produced and has proudly represented us at home and abroad. One of the first Irish artists to grace the stage of the famous Grand Ole Opry in Nashville, she is equally as well-known and respected there as she is at home. Always generous with her time and her talent, she is indeed a true professional in every sense and I wish her continued success and good health.

* * *

2012 was indeed a very important milestone, not only because of the jubilee, but also because it was then that Aidan suggested we form a new group, called the New Ramblin' Men. Aidan would be band leader, and I was filled with pride watching him manage my band for my anniversary shows. We got to spend many days planning and preparing for these gigs, and we got to travel together too, which was real fun. When he was still a child, Tom and I were reluctant to encourage Aidan to follow in our footsteps into the music industry, but by the time he was fifteen, he had already teamed up with his schoolmates, Kevin Hurson, Ronan Kane and Emmett Kane, Oliver Conlon and Rory Madden, to form his first band, the Genuine Miracles. Between them, the boys in the band had a very eclectic taste in music, mixing traditional Irish with pop, rock and country (Aidan's first love).

'It's in my blood, Ma,' he'd say to me, and I suppose it really is, because he grew up in awe of every band member I ever played with; he was always particularly taken with the drummers. Aidan's passion for music was intense – it was in his heart – and he really didn't want to even consider another career path, so we knew there would be no point in trying to stop him. So Tom and I wished him well and, I must say, he has made a real go of it.

The Miracles, as they soon became known, took to the road and proved to be a very successful young band, playing across Ireland and the UK. Their first studio recording was their version of Steve Earl's 'Galway Girl', which would be made iconic in this country by Sharon Shannon and Mundy, but the boys still talk about how they covered it first!

A few years into the Miracles, Aidan's longing to step out from behind the drum kit was realised, and since then, he has recorded four albums – *About Time*, *Born and Bred on Country Music*, *In My Mother's Footsteps* and *Overworked and Underpaid* – which helped him establish his own sound. He's a very hard-working, determined lad, and loves to get stuck in,to all sides of the business. He has been a big help to me over the years, which has also made us incredibly close.

'Ma is not only inspirational to me in my music life, but she is also inspirational to me in my everyday life,' says Aidan. 'She's my best friend; she's my wife's best friend, and I'm so proud of her. We all are. I can talk to her about anything, no matter what. She has always been so loving and caring, but let me tell you, she can scold and shout a bit too when she has to!' Aidan and I have recorded a few duets, including 'Jackson' and 'All the Road Runnin', and I must admit it was an absolute pleasure to do so.

With the New Ramblin' Men (Kenny Deveney on bass, Eugene McMullan on piano, Joe Mack on lead and steel guitar, Gordon Murray on rhythm, Chris Napier on drums and Aidan on vocals) ready to rock, we set off on a jubilee tour in April 2013, and really did take the Irish country scene by storm. Later, I found myself back in Nashville, where I was awarded the highest honour any country artist can receive. My peers hosted a tribute concert to mark my fifty years, and Lynn Anderson, Georgette Jones, Colin Ray and many more performed. LCM Promotions, a music management company with offices in New Jersey and Kildare, managed the trip. European fans were given a ten-day guided tour of Tennessee, which included my concert and visits to Dolly Parton's Dollywood, Johnny Cash's grave, Loretta Lynn's ranch, Elvis Presley's Graceland and the Country Music Hall of Fame in Nashville.

Life was showing no signs of slowing down and for an oul' doll like me, that's not a bad thing to say. Sure I wouldn't have it any other way!

Chapter Sixteen

Fans and Friendship

The best thing about fans of country music is that a lot of them become friends, not only to each other, but also to the artistes themselves. I am not completely sure why this happens, but I've been on the road for so long that familiar faces prompt conversations, which often lead to friendships. The kindness and generosity I have been shown by people from all corners of the world has blown me away, and I am so grateful to be the recipient of such kind-heartedness. Fans were especially thoughtful when my children was born, sending clothes and Babygros, and once I received a wee tractor and trailer for Mary.

You know, I still see faces that I recognise from the marquee and carnival days. And now, especially, when I perform alongside the younger generation of country stars like Lisa, Derek and Nathan, all the young ones come and ask for photos with me. I am stopped for photos when I'm out shopping, walking down the street, out for dinner or even at funerals! I'd never turn anyone away and I really enjoy chatting to people, no matter where it may be. Even small children ask me for photos, which is a lovely compliment. I'm surprised at how many of them have their own camera phones to take a selfie on!

'Do you want a photo for your mammy?' I ask some of the young ones I meet, especially teenagers, never dreaming that they want it for themselves. But they actually do. That's country music for you – it attracts fans of all ages, from all walks of life.

I often bump into the same people in the same places, and I'll know who to expect in different venues, which is why I think it has been easier for me to become close to some fans. And because I'm on the road so much, that's where my friendships are formed. I often wonder about the girls in

With my fan club manager and good friend Kathleen Cahill.

the factory who I was once so close to, and how their lives have turned out. I do run into some of them from time to time, but I have no doubt that my choice of lifestyle – travelling and spending time with my family in between – has made it difficult to maintain friendships in the more ordinary sense.

The recognition I now enjoy began back in the Country Flavour days, and it has been a way of life ever since. No matter what airport I go to, I'm sure to bump into someone who wants to share a memory of a song or a concert that means a lot to them. And for me, it's such an honour to hear it from them directly.

I do strike up friendships with fans, and I like to get to know them as much as is possible, but sometimes getting close to strangers can be challenging, as we can never fully know what goes on in each others' lives. And sometimes those who find joy in my music live very dark lives in private. I am a soft-hearted person, and when I see someone vulnerable it is hard to pass them by but this can sometimes lead to great heartache and sadness. I learned this all too well when I got to know a special lady called Lorna.

Lorna used to come to see my shows when I'd play the Irish clubs in London. She was from Peckham, and she was quite a large lady, who would sit in the front row, and after the show she would give me a big hug and a kiss. I soon realised that Lorna was keeping very strange company, maybe company that she shouldn't have been hanging out with, and I told her I was concerned.

'I'm alright Mama,' she'd say to me, but I always feared that she wasn't. She was often covered in marks, burns and bruises that she never explained.

I often gave her money for her bus home, and I even gave her my phone number, to call me if she ever felt like a chat or if she feared she might be in trouble. And one night my phone did ring. I was in the middle of my dinner, so I told one of the children to take a message, but the caller wouldn't give her name and she sounded very upset.

A few weeks later, I heard that Lorna had been murdered. It really stopped me in my tracks, and I was devastated that my biggest fear for Lorna had come true. I never found out who phoned my home that night, but I often wonder if I'd taken that call, would it have made any difference? Maybe it wasn't even Lorna ... I just have a feeling it may have been. It's something I will never find out.

Fans come in all shapes and sizes, and from all sorts of backgrounds, and I am often touched when someone tells me that a song means something to them or that my music has helped them in some way. I think that's the thing about country music – it tells a story, and it's intergenerational, so a lot of people have grown up listening to Irish country singers on the radio and it takes them back to a person or a place they hold dear.

One night in Santa Ponsa, I was at the back of the bar thinking that no one knew I was there, but the bartender sent me down a drink.

'Who's that from?' I asked the bartender.

'The band,' he said. A pop band was playing in the corner, and they had sent it over for me. 'And they'd like you to join them for a song.'

'Sure how in under God would they know who I am?' I asked. It turned out they had backed me one night in Dublin. Small world or what!

* * *

I have also developed a lengthy friendship and a respect for Fr Brian D'Arcy. In 2016, I was presented with a Lifetime Achievement Award by RTÉ at the televised Irish Country Music Awards, and it was Fr Brian who handed it over to me.

'Philomena Begley is, and always has been, the Queen of Irish country music,' said Fr Brian in his speech. 'She is equally at home singing her heart out in the parish hall, or knocking them dead on the stage at the Grand Ole Opry, and I've seen her at both. Philomena is a singer blessed with the purest and truest of voices. Everybody in the business agrees that she has this unique ability to deliver either an Irish ballad or an upbeat country song with the same heartfelt conviction. I've been lucky enough to know Philomena and her husband Tom from their earliest days of the Ramblin' Men, and over the years we've shared the good times and some-times the sad. I've been at Begley and Quinn weddings and their wakes and, through it all, Philomena soldiers on with a smile and a song for every occasion. And to let you into a little secret, I've even persuaded Philomena to join me on the altar, lending her amazing voice at our spe-cial novena nights – and she gets more money for the collection than I do! For generations of Irish music fans, Philomena has been a shining star and, for those of us lucky enough to know her well, she's been a true and constant friend. In a business notoriously difficult for women to succeed [in this country], Philomena has been a star for [more than] fifty years and believe me, she isn't about to stop anytime soon. Can I say on this special day of all, God Save the Queen!'

It was with great pride that I watched the studio audience, full of coun-try stars old and new, give me a standing ovation. I had a joke with Fr Brian between performances that night that he was trying to look at my legs, and quick as lightning, he said back:

'Sure, I've seen them often enough!'

The spokesperson of the Irish Country Music Association, Joe Finnegan, also paid tribute:

'Philomena Begley is without a doubt the doyenne of the country music scene in Ireland,' he said. 'Her career has spanned more than half a century, and she has been a truly great ambassador for the country genre right across the globe. We are delighted to be honouring a national treasure.'

Isn't it nice to be alive when you hear such things said about you, rather than people waiting till you've popped your clogs? You could easily get a big head, but sure what good is there in them all talking after you've gone and you can't hear a thing?

ANDREA BEGLEY

I grew up listening to Aunt Philomena's songs playing in the kitchen or in the car when we were out and about. One of my earliest memories of seeing her perform live was at the Galtymore in Cricklewood, London, when she took me up on stage as a bright-eyed five-year-old. I remember thinking how glamorous she was in her glitzy stage clothes, surrounded by musicians. On other, more relaxed family occasions, I remember her singing at gatherings with no band and no big lights, just Philomena unaccompanied in her true sweet style.

One of my more recent memories relates to my time on 'The Voice UK' in 2013, when Philomena came over to support me in the final of the show. When I was announced the winner, we were all invited back to a big after party with all the contestants and coaches, including Sir Tom Jones. Of course, the two of them got talking and sharing stories about their respective careers. It was a special moment having two legendary singers like Tom and Philomena together in the same room, and one that I'll certainly never forget.

If I had to sum up Philomena, I'd say she has a timeless voice, an incredible work ethic and enthusiasm for what she does. I only hope that I can follow in her footsteps and keep the Begley name as renowned with singing in the years to come.

KATHLEEN CAHILL

I first met Philly at a country festival in Wembley when I was over to see all the big USA artists like Tammy Wynette and Don Williams. After seeing Ray Lynam and Philomena sing together, I got talking to her at the record stand and we chatted for a while. I asked when she was performing next in Dublin, as I would go to see her, and we have been friends ever since. Philomena has always been there for me and my family. Nothing is ever too much for her. I remember when my mother-in-law died, Philomena had been in Kerry the night before her funeral, and she came up to Dublin at around five o'clock in the morning. We collected her and she sang at the funeral Mass at 10am. She has attended both my children's weddings and lots of other occasions, like surprising us on our twenty-fifth and fiftieth wedding anniversaries. I have found Philomena is the same person as she was when I first met her. She has never changed – she is a wonderful singer and a wonderful person, who has time for everyone. I am so proud to call her my friend.

CLIONA HAGAN

I briefly met Philomena when I was only eighteen years old, when I was singing a Shania Twain song at a marquee event on the shores of Lough Neagh. I'd heard she was going to be there, and I was a bit nervous to say the least.

'Oh my goodness, what a voice,' she said to me. 'Have you ever thought about singing more country music?'

I was classically trained and, although I knew I was going to pursue music, I didn't know what genre. Philly's son, Aidan, rang me shortly after to ask if I'd front his band, and I was really excited to be asked, but I had just been accepted into Queen's University in Belfast to study music and teaching, so I had to put everything else on hold for a few years.

When the time was right, we got it together, and it has been an absolute honour to tour with Philomena, Aidan and their band. I have learned a lot of her craft, how she engages with her audience, just observing everything she does really. I take it all on board, knowing that if I can be even half as good as her I will be doing well. She's like a second mammy to me, and she told me to treat her that way when we first started working together. She's very honest – there are no back doors in Philly and she wants the best for us all. She has such a big heart and I'm delighted to be part of her journey.

I think her success is down to the fact that she is just so grounded in every way. Fame hasn't changed her. She is still the same person, still approachable, she has no airs or graces, and that's the one big thing I think makes her so different to many others at the top of their game. No matter how talented and successful you are, connecting with your audience is key. I have learned so much and am so, so grateful to learn from the very, very best.

GEORGETTE JONES

I had the pleasure of meeting Philomena in 2009, when I was on tour in Ireland with Leona Williams, Doug Stone and Hal Ketchum. I was thrilled to get to work with her, but I had no idea how her friendship would become so special to me. I also have to thank Philomena for getting my husband and me together. She had witnessed both of us looking at each other, and even tried to talk us into speaking to the other, but one night after a show she grabbed us both by the hand and took us to the lobby. She then put our hands together and said, 'You like him and you like her so let's bond!' Now, I was embarrassed at first, but Jamie asked if he could buy me a drink and the rest is history. We've now been together eight years, thanks to Philomena giving us a shove. She has been a true friend over these years and is an amazingly talented performer. I love you Philly!

PAM LEWIS

I remember Philomena with fondness. I was doing some freelance work for the CMA during what was then called Fan Fair, held at our fairgrounds, and they asked me if I would help host our international performers. Philomena was headlining and we had a lovely time with her entourage, including her good friend Kathleen Cahill who kindly still keeps in touch with St Patrick's Day and Christmas cards. I introduced her to her first mimosa which she heartily enjoyed. I was taken with her charm, professionalism and, of course, her Irish wit.

JOE McNAMEE

I first met Philomena in the 1980s and started playing in bands with her a decade later. I am delighted to still be on the road with her and the Aidan Quinn Band all these years later. The most challenging thing about being on the road is the travelling and the sureness of a lack of sleep, which can make many people tetchy, but with Philomena the hours seem to fly by and she never changes. She takes everything in her stride and nothing will ruffle her feathers, that's for sure!

PASCHAL MOONEY

Pat McGovern introduced me to Phil by way of one of her first recordings, 'Old Ardboe', and he was so impressed with her voice that he booked her and the Country Flavour for the Mayflower Ballroom in County Leitrim.

I have had the honour of introducing Phil on concert stages all over Ireland and have always been impressed with her sheer professionalism and her down-to-earth personality, which has endeared her to generations of country fans. Her vocal range has often been underestimated and whether she is belting out 'Queen of the Silver Dollar' or ballads like 'The Way Old Friends Do', she has that unique quality of having a spellbound audience in the palm of her hand.

On a personal level, it has been an honour to know Phil and to have grown with her career spanning so many decades. Long may she continue.

LOUISE MORRISSEY

Philomena is one of my favourite singers and I am proud to call her one of my closest friends. She is the true Queen of Country, a superstar and a wonderful lady. Wishing you, Philomena, many more years of success and I always look forward to joining you on stage and for the fun and banter backstage!

Chapter Seventeen

Gold and Silver Days

Tom and I are married now just over forty years. We are both in our mid-seventies, with five grandchildren whom we are immensely proud of. Apart from having become a grandmother, life now for me hasn't changed an awful lot, as I still love to keep busy and I have no real intention of slowing down!

Our home life is very ordinary, just like it has always been. I'm in my happy place when I'm up to my elbows in dishes or wearing an apron and doing what I have to do around the house. Tom comes and goes from the farm work, and is still enjoying it the same way he has done for as long as I've known him.

I am very close to my children, and they are all so affectionate with me still, even though all three of them are married with children of their own. Aidan still loves a cuddle from his mammy, despite being over six feet tall. When they were teenagers, when we were watching TV in the evening, they'd all fight over who got to sit closest to me on the sofa, and they still would if they were all in the house at the same time! I sometimes think Aidan idolises me too much; the girls are a bit more subtle about their worship. Irish mammies and their sons! Sure we have them all ruined!

Aidan travels with me a lot these days with his own band, the Aidan Quinn Band, and I sometimes worry that he thinks I'll be around forever, but maybe every wee boy thinks that about his mother. He loves to plan ahead and is always full of ideas, but he looks out for me all the same. Sometimes he worries and asks if I want to stop or slow down, and I just say to him:

'You don't know how lucky I am to be fit and healthy enough to still do what I love doing.' And he understands, of course, as he does the thing he loves too.

I am lucky as well to get on really well with my daughter-in-law, Donna, who married Aidan in 2009. Donna is a wonderful girl, a hard worker and a lovely mammy to their two children, Joseph (5) and Ellie Rose (3), and we've developed a lovely friendship down the years. Mary married John Durnell in 2005 and they have two boys – Liam, aged nine, and Sean, who is four now, and they live just up the road from us in Aughnacloy. John is from England, so he would have different ways of doing things than us mad Irish, but he fits in nicely and is a fantastic father. So is Brian, Carol's husband – a quiet Bundoran man, who loves the craic and a bit of slagging about the football when Tyrone are playing Donegal. He and Carol were married more recently, in 2014, and they live up in Bundoran where we too have a house and I can see them a lot. Their wee Thomas came along in 2016 and was a pleasant surprise, because they'd both said that children weren't in their plan for many years. It was like there was never a child on this earth born before, as they are totally besotted with Thomas and he has brought so much joy into their lives. I stayed with Carol for a week after he was born to help her out, and I think she was sick looking at me by the time I left for home!

A playful hug at home with Mary and Carol.

Mary tells me her announcement that she was pregnant with Liam was a nerve-wracking experience. I don't know why she was so nervous! We were delighted for her and were hoping for this news, so she had no need to be so afraid.

'Even though I am a grown woman and was married, I was still nervous to tell my parents because it meant they knew how it had happened,' laughs Mary. 'When we were growing up, kissing on the TV was turned over, so I suppose I was a bit embarrassed. Mammy had to tell Daddy, and when I asked her was he okay with it, she laughed and said, "Of course he was – how do you think you lot came along?"'

When Mary's baby Liam was due, I was booked to be in Spain with Declan Nerney, as part of his Hooley in the Sun Tour. I was on standby the whole time and I couldn't settle at all, so I flew home for two nights and got there in time for the birth. Tour or no tour, I couldn't have missed the birth of my first grandchild, not for the world.

Aidan's announcement that he was going to be a father was a bit more creative! We had a bull on our farm that wasn't 'producing the goods', so to speak. Around the same time we noticed this, Aidan landed in to us with a bottle of whiskey he had bought en route from Paudge Quinn's bar. He put the whiskey down on the kitchen table in front of his father and me and made his grand statement.

'At least there's one bull working about this house anyway,' he said, and we knew exactly what he meant.

* * *

On a day-to-day basis, I lead what is sometimes a very ordinary, simple life. In the morning, it's just me and Tom, and we potter about like any other couple at our stage in life. I make Tom his breakfast, and find things to do around the house. I just can't stay still, and will always make sure I'm busy, be it clearing out kitchen drawers or washing clothes: I enjoy being at home and I don't really leave the house unless I have to. I sometimes wonder if I did want to go and do something else, who I would do it with. I look at my daughters and how they have maintained a circle of friends from their schooldays. They go out at least three times a year for either lunch or dinner and a catch-up, always keeping in touch. I think with my line of business, I never really had the chance to make that connection, or to build strong female friendships. For most of my life, I've had to be 'one of the lads' on tour, and I had to just take it in my stride – I didn't really have a choice!

I'm an old-fashioned housewife now in many ways: I love to bake soda bread, to do the ironing and to watch the soaps in the evenings. I love 'Coronation Street' and 'Emmerdale', and would always catch up with them if I've missed them. I'm not that fussed on 'Eastenders', but I'll still watch it the odd time, just to make sure I'm not missing out on anything exciting! I so enjoy the soaps, and the only time I really do sit down and relax is when I'm watching TV. I would watch 'The Late Late Show', and I'm delighted to see so many country stars being showcased there now. It wasn't always the way, and it's an advantage to local musicians to have that nationwide outlet and support.

As far as hobbies go, I try and read a bit from time to time, and I do prefer a proper print book over reading anything online, because technology and I don't really work that well together. Yes, I have an iPad, but sure, I haven't a notion what to do with it! I have a Facebook account, but don't ask me to do much more than scroll through it, and I often joke about the two magic phones I have: one for the south of Ireland and one for the north, and they just about text and I can make calls. That's it. I did get a fancier phone once, but was so baffled by it that I prefer to stick to my wee simple Nokia.

At home in Galbally, we don't have too many visitors these days, now that the children have grown up and have their own places. When we were younger, we may have had more people around and the odd party, but it was always very off-the-cuff – we were never the type to show off or have big dinner parties. Anyone who comes to our home is always made welcome and, while Tom and I both like our privacy and our own space, it's always nice to see a warm, familiar face call in for a chat and a cup of tea.

Our holidays every year are spent in a place we love called Benalmádena, in Spain. We stay in the same hotel, close to McGuinness's Bar, and we may

Catching up with Frankie McBride, Big Tom and Gene Stuart (RIP) in Bundoran, November 2015.

as well be in Bundoran, because I always end up singing in the bar every night we are there! There is always someone to ask me up for a song, and I've performed with every type of musician, from Polish bands to Maltese bands. You just never know who you might meet, and I'm always up for the challenge and willing to give it a go!

Tom loves to go to O'Malley's for breakfast every morning in Spain, and in the afternoon we will walk the beaches together and enjoy the peace and change of scenery.

* * *

Even in my gold and silver days, I'm lucky that I still get many opportunities to travel for work, and I love to be a part of the Spanish events organised by Enjoy Travel a few times a year. I've performed on these tours many times, with Nathan Carter, Mick Flavin and Declan Nerney, and more recently with Paul Claffy and the Three Amigos.

With James McGarrity, I loved participating in the annual Queens of Country Tour, which ran between 2007 and 2011. This featured stars like Lynn Anderson, Georgette Jones, Louise Morrissey, Dee Reilly, Jeannie Seely, the late Billie Jo Spears and Leona Williams. I love working with these ladies. It's always such a memorable experience, as we have so much in common. We each love country music, and entertain in our own unique ways wherever we go.

So many proud moments! And I can honestly say I have no regrets, which I think is a very healthy state of mind to be in at my age. Things always worked out for the better. So, if life doesn't take you on the path you thought it would, it's mostly because you have something still to learn. I have been very lucky in life: I have my health and I have a fantastic, supportive husband. Tom is old stock; he loves family life and he loves farming, and we never put pressure on each other to do anything we didn't want to or didn't feel was for the best. I'm sure it wasn't always easy on him as I travelled the world for my job, but I think his laid-back attitude helped with that. Plus he has a strong character and is a remarkable father. I couldn't ask for more.

If I had to give up my music I would die, simple as that. It's my life, and I don't know any different as I muse here during my fifty-fifth year in the business. I have met some fabulous people along the way, far too many to mention in one book – my memory isn't what it used to be, so forgive me for not naming everyone. I'm not getting any younger and it's par for the course that the old brain gets a bit muddled when it comes to naming names!

I do forget the words to songs sometimes, but that has nothing to do with age – it's just me and I can't help it! In fact, I've always forgotten the words to songs, and have just asked the audience to help me along. And you know, they always do. I just talk away to the crowd, even during songs, and it wouldn't be the same without that contact. I suppose you could say that it's part of my act.

Every time I step on stage now, I feel proud of how far I have come, and I will never take any of my success for granted. But I have worked mightily hard for many years to be able to keep doing what I love, and it's only as I get older that I have really begun to appreciate my life and allowed the pride in.

* * *

Nothing can make you prouder than your own children though, and I take so much comfort from how Mary, Aidan and Carol have become such fine adults, and parents in their own right. Our grandchildren have brought immense joy, happiness and energy into our homes. I'm very much a 'hands-on' granny, doing the odd school run or looking after them for a few hours, helping to organise birthday parties and sing 'Happy Birthday' as they blow out their candles. It's very different being a grandparent, because you can enjoy them to the full and then hand them back!

They all call me 'Ma', because that's what they hear their parents calling me, and it has stuck, beginning with Liam, the only grandchild for four years, and then the others following suit. Mary told me that one day Liam was asked at school could he sing like his 'nanny' and he asked, 'Who's Nanny?' It's not a term any of them can relate to at all.

Liam was watching the BBC show 'Keepin 'er Country' recently when a little girl, who was around his age, was asked who her idol was, and she answered 'Philomena Begley'.

Liam turned to his mother and said:

'Is she for real? Is my *Ma* her idol?'

He does love a bit of country music himself now. His favourite is Nathan Carter, so when Mary takes him along to a concert that Nathan and I are performing in, that's when his Ma becomes cool!

I hear from each of my children by telephone at least five times a day. They don't live too far away, but we really like to keep up with each other. The habit probably stems from all the times I was away on the road and I would phone them as often as I could. It might seem a bit excessive, but it's just what we are used to. I can tell without looking at the phone which one of them is calling, just by the time of day!

'My husband thinks it's very strange that we talk so much on a day-to-day basis,' says Mary. 'He phones his mother in England about once a fortnight and doesn't see her very often, yet Mammy is just down the road and the first thing I do when I get up in the morning is phone her to see how she is, and we update each other throughout the day. If I know she's had a late night, I'll leave it until she has a bit of time to lie in, but chances are she'll ring me by a certain time of day if I haven't made the phone call first.'

As I reach the age of seventy-five, I often wonder if there is anything else in my career that I would still like to do. I still have many, many ideas churning around that I would like to pursue, but I won't say too much

A proud day at Mary's wedding.

about them, as I'd rather just get stuck in and do them. I loved making the video for 'All the Road Running' with Aidan and a few friends and, as I said before, Aidan is always coming up with new suggestions, so I don't think there will ever be a time that I'll be idle for too long.

I think my only problem is that I don't know how to say no. It's very hard to do, especially when there is a charity element to a request. I'm still always on the go and my diary, which, believe it or not, I manage myself, is never empty for long.

People often ask me if I will ever retire, or what I plan to do when I retire, but the very word doesn't sit well with me. Why would I stop doing something I love so much? I am incredibly blessed to still feel I have something to offer, and I'm even more blessed that those on the receiving end agree with me. I love to work with the younger artists, like Mike Denver, Nathan Carter and, of course, Cliona Hagan, who has toured with me and Aidan's band lately. In fact, just as I finished writing this book, I recorded a new song by Derek Ryan, called 'My Life, My Music, My Memories', to celebrate my seventy-fifth birthday. I strongly believe keeping that company keeps me young!

If I could sum up my life in one word, I would have to say 'contentment', and what a way to be! Lately, I often think back to my childhood days in Pomeroy: doing the grocery delivery run with my uncle Eugene; doing one, penny concerts in Harte's Yard; wheeling my wee brother Kieran around the town and showing him off in his pram; hearing my father sing songs around the fire; the smell of smoke and the sounds of laughter coming from our kitchen on a daily basis; sneaking up the stairs when I'd come in from a dance and dreading the creaky floorboard; careless summers spent at Gortnagarn, and winters sliding down hills in the ice and snow. They were idyllic days, and maybe that's why I never felt the urge to live any where else. I am surrounded by loving memories of a blissful childhood in a village in County Tyrone.

My motto in life is to keep doing what makes me happy, and for me that's to keep singing and performing. It's a good way to live life: find a way to make a living that fills you up and makes you want to keep bettering yourself. Maybe I'm one of the lucky ones for whom it worked out that way. I do know in my heart, though, that as a person I have never changed from the girl I was back then. I haven't been hardened by life, nor have I taken anything for granted. My sisters and brothers can see that too. To them and to everyone, I'm still Philly from Pomeroy and that will never change, no matter how many big fancy stadiums I play, and no matter how many celebrities I meet along the way.

I'll give this up when it gives me up. And I hope that won't be any time soon.

Discography

Over a long and busy career, I've recorded hundreds of songs. Maybe a few have escaped mention below, so this is as complete as possible. Codes in brackets indicate the catalogue numbers assigned to original pressings or releases.

OLD CROSS CÉILÍ BAND EARLY SINGLES, 1968
Come, Me Little Son
The Box That It Came In
Old Ardboe
A Village in County Tyrone

TRUCK DRIVIN' WOMAN: RELEASE RECORDS, 1972 (BRL4030)
Ramblin' Man
Truck Drivin' Woman
I'll Be All Smiles Tonight
I Really Think I'm Crying
How Can I Face Tomorrow?
Here Today and Gone Tomorrow
Never Again
Darling Are You Ever Coming Home?
Philadelphia Lawyer
A Village in County Tyrone
Come, Me Little Son
Old Ardboe

THE TWO OF US (with Ray Lynam): RELEASE RECORDS, 1973 (BRLP 4035)

We Go Together
Never Grow Cold
Just Someone I Used to Know
Silver Sandals
You're the One I Can't Live Without
Daddy Was an Old Time Preacher Man
We're Locking Up Each Souvenir
All These Little Things
Seeing Eye to Eye
We Believe in Each Other
Jeannie's Afraid of the Dark
You Never Were Mine

TOGETHER ... AGAIN! (with Ray Lynam): RELEASE RECORDS, 1974 (BRLP 4057)

You and Me, Him and Her
If You Were Mine
Mr & Mrs Used to Be
That's When My Baby Sings His Song
In the Vine
Anything's Better than Nothing
My Elusive Dreams
We Found It
Take My Hand
We Love to Sing about Jesus
Heaven Help the People
We've Run Out of Tomorrows

MEET THE QUEEN OF COUNTRY MUSIC: TOP SPIN, 1974 (TSLP71)

Texas in My Heart

False Eyelashes

Song I Can Sing

Crying Steel Guitar

I Apologise

Lucky Old Me

Honky Tonkitis

Where Do Babies Go?

I Love You Honey

You Never Were Mine

If I Had the Right

Truck Driver's Sweetheart

INTRODUCES HER RAMBLIN' MEN: TOP SPIN, 1975 (TSLP76)

Sweet Baby Jane

Cherro Moana Marie

Wildwood Flower

What's Your Mama's Name?

Laugh with Me

Today, Tomorrow and Forever

Cinco de Mayo

Daddy Dumplin'

Little Piece of Heaven

There Goes My Heart Again

Hello Mary Lou

Truck Driver's Sweetheart

BLANKET ON THE GROUND: TOP SPIN, 1975 (TSLP82)

Blanket on the Ground

If God Can Forgive You

Mama Spank

Stand beside Me

Where Is the Broken Heart?

Sleep My Baby

They Don't Make 'Em Like My Daddy
You Don't Need to Move a Mountain
Satin Sheets
Three Ways to Love You
Poor Sweet Baby
I'm Your Country Girl

QUEEN OF THE SILVER DOLLAR: TOP SPIN, 1976 (TSLP86)

Queen of the Silver Dollar
Why Me Lord?
Storms Never Last
Burn the Roadside Tavern Down
It's a Long Way from Heaven
Nitro Express
Mexico
Hold on Woman
Wait a Little Longer, Please Jesus
Country I'm A Coming
Don't Make Me Go to School
Hear the Family Sing

IRISH COUNTRY QUEEN: TOP SPIN, 1976 (TSLP90)

Grandma Whistled
Medals for Mother
My Mother's Home
County Tyrone
Can I Sleep in Your Arms?
Light in the Window
Once around the Dance Floor
Irish Eyes
Tipperary Town
How Great Thou Art
41st Street Lonely Heart Club
Lonesome End of the Line

TRUCKIN' QUEEN: TOP SPIN 1977 (TSLP98)

Route 65 to Nashville
In God We Trust
Ravishing Ruby
Big Mac
Big Wheel Cannon Ball
Highway Man
Long-Legged Truck Driver
Old Ben
Roll on Big Mama
Runaway Truck
Truck Driving Mother

NASHVILLE COUNTRY: TOP SPIN, 1978 (TSLP110)

No Man Is a Mountain
Mama's and Daddy's Little Girl
Some Old Rainy Morning
I'll Be a Lady Tomorrow (*also known as* I'm Gonna Be Your Woman Tonight)
I Wonder Where I'll Find You Out Tonight
Get a Little Hurt Out
The Umbrella Song
Catfish John
Let the Teardrops Fall on Me
Seeing You with Her
The Only Man-Made Thing in Heaven
Tonight I'll Throw a Party of My Own

FIRESIDE COUNTRY: TOP SPIN, 1979 (TSLP113)

Take Me Along
I Just Wanna Be a Country Girl
A Fool Like Me
Down River Road
The Shoe Goes on the Other Foot Tonight
It Must Be You
Heartache Follow Me
Billy Jo

Mamas Don't Let Your Babies Grow Up to Be Cowboys
How Can I Help You Forgive Me
San Antonio Rose
Yes Mam He Found Me in a Honky Tonk

THE BEST OF PHILOMENA BEGLEY: K-TEL, 1979 (KLP049)

SCOTS 'N' IRISH: BGS, 1979 (ITV476)

The Big Wheel Cannonball
Flower of Scotland
Rose of Mooncoin
Mull of Kintyre
The Way Old Friends Do
Mama's and Daddy's Little Girl
Making Love to You Is Just Like Eating Peanuts
Cliffs of Dooneen
Come by the Hills
I'm Crying My Heart Out Over You
That's What Your Love Means to Me
Cottage on the Hill
Everything I Touch Turns to Sugar
Scotland Again

PHILOMENA'S COUNTRY: TOP SPIN, 1980 (SSLP502)

I Don't Believe I'll Fall in Love Today
One Night of Cheating
Sweet Baby Jane
Foolin' Around
Daydreams about Night Things
The Triangle Song
Faded Love
Everything I've Always Wanted
God If I Could Only Write Your Love Song
I Can't Keep My Hands off You
If This Is What Love's All About
Okie from Muskogee

MY KIND OF COUNTRY: TOP SPIN, 1982 (SSLP508)

Big Four-Poster Bed
You Can't Make Love by Yourself
The Buck Dance
Country Girl
Excuse Me (I Think I've Got a Heartache)
Darlin' It's Yours
I Don't Feel Like a Movie Tonight
I Fall to Pieces
Back to Back
CB Window
Don't Make My Heart Ache Tonight
Teardrops Are Smarter Than You Think

COUNTRY SCENES (COMPILATION): K-TEL, 1983 (KTEL310)

YOU'RE IN MY HEART: RITZ, 1984 (RITZLP026)

Sentimental Old You
Honky Tonkin'
Have I Told You Lately That I Love You
Pull the Covers over Me
Old Flames
Deportees
The Way Old Friends Do
Ease the Fever
One of Those Days
Jealous Heart
Dancing Your Memory Away
Daddy's Side of the Bed
You Don't Know Love

SIMPLY DIVINE (with Ray Lynam), RITZ, 1985 (RITZLP0028)

Simply Divine
Together Alone
Near You
Don't Step Over an Old Love

Making Plans
Sweetest of All
I'll Never Need Another You
She Sang the Melody
Long as We're Dreaming
We're Gonna Hold On
Fire of Two Old Flames
How's the World Treating You
Jeannie's Afraid of the Dark

MORE ABOUT LOVE: RITZ, 1987 (RITZLP040)

That's More about Love
Grandpa
Mama He's Crazy
Standing in Line
Another Chance
Sailor
Captured By Love
I'll Be Faithful to You
It Only Hurts For a Little While
Memories Are Made of This
One Love at a Time
Real Men Don't Eat Quiche

SILVER ANNIVERSARY: RITZ, 1989 (RITZLP046)

The Key's in the Mailbox
Leaving on Your Mind
Here Today and Gone Tomorrow
Queen of the Silver Dollar
Rose of My Heart
Blanket on the Ground
Behind the Footlights
Truck Drivin' Woman
Jeannie's Afraid of the Dark
One Is One Too Many
Red Is the Rose

Galway Bay
Dark Island
Old Ardboe

IN HARMONY (with Mick Flavin): RITZ, 1991 (RITZLP061)
No Love Left
Just Between You and Me
I'm Wasting Your Time, You're Wasting Mine
Till a Tear Becomes a Rose
Always, Always
We're Strangers Again
We'll Get Ahead Someday
All You've Got to Do Is Dream
Daisy Chain
Don't Believe Me I'm Lying
You Can't Break the Chains of Love
Let's Pretend We're Not Married Tonight
How Can I Help You Forgive Me
Somewhere Between

REFLECTIONS: K-TEL, 1992 (KLP310)
Have You Ever Been Lonely?
Hillbilly Girl with the Blues
Daddy and Home
I'm So Afraid of Losing You
Too Young
Little Grey Home in the West
Heartaches
Carolina Moon
A Pal Like Mother
After All these Years
God, I Love You
My Tears Will Tell My Heart
When Two Worlds Collide
Breath in My Body

THE WAY OLD FRIENDS DO (with Margo): SHARPE MUSIC, 1996 (PADDYCD17)

Mother, May I?

God's Colouring Book

Gold And Silver Days

I See God

He Took Your Place

Wishful Thinking

Crystal Chandeliers

Golden Memories

The Way Old Friends Do

Colour Me Blue

Darling Days

There'll Be Love

Husband Hunting

Hallelujah In My Heart (featuring Liz Anderson And Skeeter Davis)

TODAY: 2003 (privately released)

Still Feeling Blue

The Song from Way Back Then

The Gambler

Woman in the Moon

Just Because I'm a Woman

Only Yesterday

Scotland Again

Blue House Painted White

The Cottage on the Dungannon Road

Don't Tell Mama (I Was Drinking)

Go On and Go

I Love You Enough to Let You Go

Leaving Houston Blue

Que Sera Sera (Whatever Will Be, Will Be)

Why Can't He Be with You

VILLAGE IN COUNTY TYRONE: H&H MUSIC, 2003 (HHCD231)

To Hear the Family Sing

Grandma Whistled

Medals for Mothers

I Don't Believe I'll Fall in Love Today

Lucky Old Me

Grandpa Tell Us about the Good Old Days

Yes Mam He Found Me in a Honky Tonk

I Love You Honey

Big Four-Poster Bed

Our Wedding Day

No Man Is a Mountain

Mama's and Daddy's Little Girl

Come, Me Little Son

Daddy's Side of the Bed

Jealous Heart

A Picture of Me

Where Do Babies Go?

Come by the Hills

Old Ardboe

Mama He's Crazy

A Village in County Tyrone

A Pal Like Mother

Walkin', Talkin', Cryin', Barely Beatin' Broken Heart

Crying Steel Guitar

One Is One Too Many

I'm Crying My Heart Out over You

Some Ol' Rainy Morning

My Mother's Home

County Tyrone

The Bed You Made for Me

Honky Tonkitis

Cottage on the Hill

Can I Sleep in Your Arms?

Light in the Window

Route 65 to Nashville
You Can't Make Love by Yourself
You Are the One I Can't Live Without (with Ray Lynam)
Still Feeling Blue
A Song I Can Sing
In God We Trust

ONCE AROUND THE DANCE FLOOR: H&H MUSIC, 2003 (HHCD232)

The Song from Way Back Then
Honky Tonkin'
Ease the Fever
Blanket on the Ground
Once around the Dance Floor
Jose Cuervo
I'm Gonna Be Your Woman Tonight (*also known as* I'll Be a Lady Tomorrow)
False Eyelashes
Irish Eyes
Buck Dance
The Big Wheel Cannonball
Galway Bay
Little Grey Home in the West
Carolina Moon
Take Me Along
The Gambler
Memories Are Made of This
I Just Wanna Be a Country Girl
Truck Drivin' Woman
Flower of Scotland
I Wonder Where I'll Find You out Tonight
One Night of Cheating
A Fool Like Me
Every Second
If I Had the Right
Dancing Your Memory Away
Jeannie's Afraid Of the Dark

My Elusive Dreams (with Ray Lynam)
Sweet Baby Jane
Cherro Moana Marie
Wildwood Flower
What's Your Mama's Name?
Laugh With Me
Today, Tomorrow and Forever
Cinco de Mayo
Daddy Dumplin'
There Goes My Heart Again
Hello Mary Lou
Truck Driver's Sweetheart

RED IS THE ROSE: H&H MUSIC, 2004 (HHCD233)
Pull the Covers over Me
Down River Road
Dark Island
Just One More Time
Queen of the Silver Dollar
The Shoe Goes on the Other Foot Tonight
Cliffs of Dooneen
Here Today and Gone Tomorrow
Country Girl
Tipperary Town
Leaving on My Mind
Home I'll Be
Excuse Me (I Think I've Got a Heartache)
Darling It's Yours
Foolin' Around
Get a Little Hurt Out
Bright Lights and Country Music
Start Living Again
Bing Bang Boom
How Great Thou Art
What's Wrong with the Way We're Doing it Now?
Red Is the Rose

Fallin' For You
Daydreams about Night Things
I Don't Feel Like a Movie Tonight
The Woman in the Moon
Just Because I Am a Woman
I Fall to Pieces
The Triangle Song
The Umbrella Song
Country I'm A Coming
Storms Never Last
I Burnt the Little Riverside Tavern Down
It's a Long Way from Heaven
The Nitro Express
Mexico
Hold on Woman
Wait a Little Longer, Please Jesus
Only Yesterday
Ravishing Ruby
Isle of Innisfree
Why Me Lord?

THE WAY OLD FRIENDS DO: H&H MUSIC, 2004 (HHCD234)
Sentimental Old You
Have I Told You Lately That I Love You
Too Young
Heartaches
It Must Be You
Breath in My Body
The Way Old Friends Do
Look at Us
Rose of My Heart
Gold and Silver Days
Old Flames
Last Rose of Summer
I'm So Afraid of Losing You
One of Those Days

That's More about Love Than I Wanted To Know
Real Men Don't Eat Quiche
Sailor
Deportees
Only Yesterday
Behind the Footlights
I Love a Ramblin' Man
I Really Think I'm Crying
Darling Are You Ever Coming Home
How Can I Face Tomorrow
You and Me, Him and Her (with Ray Lynam)
Never Again
Truck Driver's Sweetheart
You Never Were Mine
I've Got Texas in My Heart
Don't Make Me Go to School
Heartaches Follow Me
Ballad of Billy Joe
The Key's in the Mailbox
Faded Love
Rose of Mooncoin
When Two Worlds Collide
Mull of Kintyre
Scotland Again
Blue House Painted White
The Cottage on the Dungannon Road

LIVE IN DUNDEE: 1989 (re-released as DVD, H&H MUSIC, 2007) (HHDVD808)

Queen of the Silver Dollar
Truck Drivin' Woman
Sentimental Old You
After All Those Years
Isle of Innisfree
A Pal Like Mother
I'm So Afraid of Losing You

Route 65 to Nashville
Dark Island
Hillbilly Girl with the Blues
One Drink Is One Too Many
I'll Be Faithful to You
How Great Thou Art
Blanket on the Ground

I'LL ONLY GIVE THIS UP WHEN IT GIVES ME UP: H&H MUSIC, 2011 (HHCD315)

I Guess to Pieces
Mama Knows the Highway
The Last Supper
Pass Me By (If You're Only Passing Through)
It's Been a Long Time
Life's Storybook Cover
Where Ya Coming From?
Driving
The Wind beneath My Wings
I Love You Enough to Let You Go
Don't Tell Mama (I Was Drinking)
Only Yesterday
Go On and Go
Blue Jean Country Queen
Que Sera Sera (Whatever Will Be, Will Be)
Listen to the Children
Family Tree
I'll Only Give This up When It Gives Me Up (DVD Biography)

FROM THEN TILL NOW: H&H MUSIC, 2012 (HHCD320)

I Love a Ramblin' Man
Come, Me Little Son
A Village in County Tyrone
Old Ardboe
Truck Drivin' Woman
Mama's and Daddy's Little Girl

Here Today and Gone Tomorrow
My Elusive Dreams (with Ray Lynam)
Jeannie's Afraid of the Dark (with Ray Lynam)
You and Me, Him and Her (with Ray Lynam)
False Eyelashes
I Love You Honey
Crying Steel Guitar
Lucky Old Me
Honky Tonkitis
You Never Were Mine
Where Do Babies Go?
I've Got Texas in My Heart
Queen of the Silver Dollar
Blanket on the Ground
Today, Tomorrow or Forever (with Dan O'Hara)
Once around the Dance Floor
Light in the Window
What's Wrong with the Way We're Doing It Now?
Down River Road
Wait a Little Longer, Please Jesus
Route 65 to Nashville
The Umbrella Song
Jose Cuervo
The Triangle Song
Big Four-Poster Bed
Medals for Mothers
Blue Jean Country Queen
The Way Old Friends Do
Honky Tonkin'
Deportees
Pull the Covers over Me
Red Is the Rose
Sentimental Ol' You
One Love at a Time
The Key's in the Mailbox
Gold and Silver Days

Dark Island
Galway Bay
Home I'll Be
The Song from Way Back Then
The Last Supper
It's Been a Long Time
A Tribute to Billie Jo
God, If I Could Only Write Your Love Song
Wildwood Flower

50 YEARS OF MUSIC AND MEMORIES: H&H MUSIC, 2013 (HHDVD813)

Medley: I Love a Ramblin' Man/Truck Drivin' Woman/Blanket on the Ground/ Queen of the Silver Dollar
Medley: Old Ardboe/Come, Me Little Son/Here Today and Gone Tomorrow
Sailor
The Way Old Friends Do (with Daniel O'Donnell)
Jackson (with Aidan Quinn)
The Key's in the Mailbox
A Village in County Tyrone
Bláth Mhachaire Ailligh O (sung by Andrea Begley)
Deportees
Only Yesterday
How Great Thou Art
The Umbrella Song
You're the One I Can't Live Without (with Ray Lynam)
What's Wrong with the Way We're Doing It Now?
I Really Think I'm Crying
A Tribute to Billie Jo
Blanket on the Ground
All the Road Running (with Aidan Quinn)
I Ain't Over the Hill

HOW I LOVE THEM OLD SONGS: H&H MUSIC, 2013 (HHCD325)

I Ain't over the Hill

How I Love Them Old Songs

Burning an Old Memory

Waltz through a Lifetime with You

Sorry

Taste of Life

Raglan Road

The Story I Tell You Is True

The Star

Your Health Is Your Wealth

Don't Tell Me this Is How the Story Ends

Heartaches by the Number

It Only Hurts For a Little While

All the Road Running (with Aidan Quinn)

I'm Going to California

Sentimental Journey

Country Girls Never Grow Old (with Debbie Moore and Carrie Moore)

THE COMPLETE DUET COLLECTION (with Ray Lynam): H&H MUSIC, 2014 (HHCD257). Includes THE TWO OF US, 1973; TOGETHER ... AGAIN! 1974; SIMPLY DIVINE, 1985

Awards and Accolades

* First Irish female artiste to sing at the Grand Ole Opry, Nashville, Tennessee
* A European Gold Star Award
* British Country Music Hall of Fame inductee, 2013
* Top Female Vocalist, 1985: British Country Music Association Annual Awards
* 6 Grand Ole Opry appearances
* 9 No. 1 singles
* 12 Wembley Country Music Festivals
* 25 albums
* Sold out tours of Ireland, UK, Europe, America and Australia
* 55 years in show business (as of 11 May 2017)

About the Authors

Multi-award-winning singer **Philomena Begley** is an Irish country star whose international career in show business spans fifty-five years. She lives in Galbally, County Tyrone, with her husband Tom, and she is a proud mother of three and a grandmother of five. When not entertaining the crowds, Philomena enjoys spending time with her family, following Tyrone GAA and baking.

Emma Heatherington is a bestselling author from Donaghmore, County Tyrone. Her novels include the UK Top Ten Amazon Kindle hit *The Legacy of Lucy Harte* (HarperImpulse, HarperCollins, 2017), which is also translated internationally. Emma has also penned three stage musicals and over sixty educational short films and plays. She lives with her partner Jim McKee, and together they have five children, aged from two to twenty-one years old.

Acknowledgements

PHILLY THANKS:

Thanks to my loving family, Tom Quinn, Mary Durnell, Aidan Quinn and Carol Gillespie, for all their support and contributions to this book; to Kathleen Cahill for her long-lasting friendship and ongoing support; to Michael, Ivan, Aoife, Ruth and Geraldine at The O'Brien Press for their belief and vision; to Anthony and Joan Loughman for access to their extensive archives; to my brothers and sisters, Mary, Annette, Angela, Plunkett, Margaret and Kieran; to all the media, both local and international, for their coverage and enthusiasm for so, so many years; thanks to Steve Brink for all his support, knowledge, contributions and enthusiasm for this book, especially his detailed help on the discography and photo archives – it is much appreciated. To all the venues who have hosted me and my bands, and to all those friends and family members gone before me who inspired so many stories from my lifetime – I remember you often and you are always in my heart. Thank you to my fans, both old and new, who have turned up, stood by me, sung with me, cheered, laughed and danced along the way – let the good times keep rolling! Finally, thanks to Emma Heatherington for all her expertise, friendship and creativity, and for helping to put my many experiences into words. I've enjoyed it immensely.

EMMA THANKS:

Thanks to Tom Quinn, Mary Durnell, Aidan Quinn and Carol Gillespie, and the wider Begley family, for helping answer my many questions on Philomena's amazing life. To my own family: my partner, Jim McKee, and our children, Jordyn, Jade, Dualta, Adam and Sonny James – thanks as always for putting up with me spending so much time at the laptop, and for keeping the home fires burning. A big thanks to all at The O'Brien Press, especially Michael O'Brien, for entrusting me with this project, and Aoife Walsh for all her direction and for helping me pull the book into shape. To Anthony Loughman – your archives were priceless! Thanks for sharing them with me and for answering messages on Facebook at record speed. To John and Teresa O'Neill for your knowledge and hospitality; to Eamonn Holmes and Gloria Hunniford for helping me collate that fab UTV story; to John Conway, Anne Conway, Irene McKee, Sharon Shannon and Shunie Crampsey for help with song lyric permissions; to Kathleen Cahill for rooting for me and for having the best memory (not to mention the best Little Black Book of contacts!). And, of course, a massive thanks to the Queen of Country Music herself, for suggesting my input and for lots of fun times along the way, from Donegal to Monaghan to Dublin and who knows where next! It's been an absolute honour to play a part in your autobiography; it's been fun, it's been insightful, it's been emotional and it's a memory I will always treasure. May you reign for many years to come.

OUT NOW!

New single, 'My Life, My Music, My Memories',
available in all good music shops and online.

H&H Music

HHCD113

www.handhmusic.co.uk

The official memoir of Margo
O'Donnell, legendary Irish
country music singer. For fifty
years now the name 'Margo'
has been synonymous with
everything that is positive and
enriching in Irish country music.
This is the story of her life, the
successes and difficult times, in
her own words.

Hardback ISBN: 978-1-84717-674-5

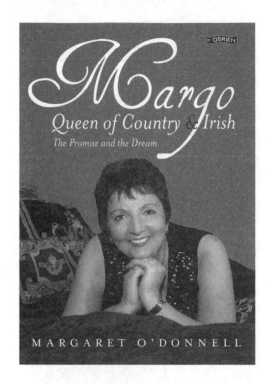

In Ireland, Daniel O'Donnell
is more than just a singing star:
he has reached the status of
'national treasure'. It has been a
long journey for the boy from
Kincasslagh, County Donegal,
and in this updated autobiography, he tells his story with his
customary sense of humour and
down-to-earth charm.

Hardback ISBN: 978-1-84717-967-8

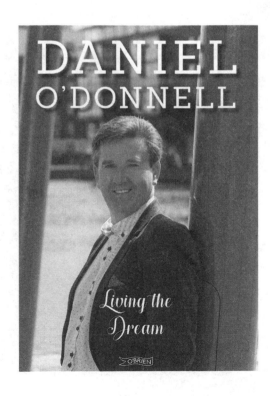

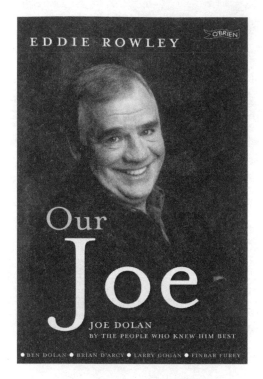

Read the story of Joe Dolan through his own interviews and the memories and anecdotes of his family that vividly bring to life the essence of Joe.

Paperback ISBN: 978-1-84717-219-8

Marie Duffy is the undisputed queen of Irish dancing: she has trained more world champions than any other teacher, and has been Michael Flatley's right-hand woman for twenty years.
Get a behind-the-scenes view of the world of professional Irish dance, and Marie's own fascinating and inspiring life.

Hardback ISBN: 978-1-84717-926-5

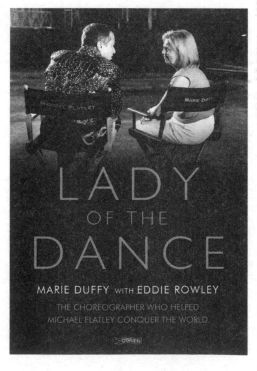